Dowse Your Way to Psychic Power

ANTHONY TALMAGE

ISBN-10: 1497590108
ISBN-13: 978-1497590106

FOREWORD

In 1991, when her daughter's rare, hand-carved harp was stolen, Associate Professor Elizabeth Lloyd Mayer, clinical supervisor at the University of California, Berkeley's Psychology Clinic, did something extraordinary for a dyed-in-the-wool scientific thinker. After the police failed to turn up any leads, a friend suggested she call a dowser, who specialized in finding lost objects. With nothing to lose—and almost as a joke—Dr. Mayer agreed. Within two days, and without leaving his Arkansas home 1500 miles away, the dowser located the exact California street coordinates where the harp was found. What followed turned Dr Mayer's familiar world of science and rational thinking upside down. Deeply shaken, yet driven to understand what had happened, Mayer began a fourteen-year journey of discovery which ended in her writing her bestseller 'Extraordinary Knowing' that explores what science has to say about this episode and countless other 'inexplicable' phenomena. From Sigmund Freud's writings on telepathy to secret CIA experiments on remote viewing, from leading-edge neuroscience to the strange world of quantum physics, Dr. Mayer researched a wealth of credible and fascinating information about the psychic world where the mind seems to trump the laws of nature. This book you are holding now goes one step further – it will make you part of this world and this world will become part of you.

CONTENTS

Dowse [1] |douz| - To search for or discover something by intuition or sixth sense: *water is easy to dowse for; he dowsed a spiral of energy on the stone.* To search for underground water, minerals, etc., using a divining rod; to divine

Psychic |'sy kik| - Relating to or denoting faculties or phenomena that are apparently inexplicable by natural laws, esp. involving telepathy or clairvoyance : *psychic powers* (of a person) appearing or considered to have powers beyond the normal five senses: *I could sense it—I must be psychic.*

PREFACE

So you want to enhance your psychic abilities. Dowsing is the way to do it. Dowsing is like that theoretical wormhole in space that connects far away places - it enables you to jump straight there without the tedious business of travelling thousands of light years and waiting several lifetimes. Dowsing is a bridge to the information field 'out there' which contains everything you will ever need to become a powerful psychic. The fact that you are reading this means that you are on the edge of that wormhole in space but to get to the other side there are certain steps you have to take and I am here to help you take them and make sure you arrive safely.

Our journey will take us though territory containing the mystical and the paranormal. By the time we reach our destination we will have encountered angels, spirit guides, elementals, ghosts, poltergeists and entities that dwell in other dimensions. We will have looked at precognition, retro-cognition, trance states, possession, past lives and re-incarnation. We will learn how to communicate with animals and plants, how to move energy from one place to another and how to go back, and forward, in time. As we travel you will learn what psychic skills are available to you and which are the ones that will make you a unique 'psychic.' But none of this can happen without dowsing. Without dowsing we are going nowhere; so the first thing we have to do is find out all we need to know about this ancient art and how we can turn it into that short-cut to psychic power.

The word 'Dowsing' falls far short of encapsulating the mind-boggling possibilities which it offers. I've tried to find other, more appropriate words but there just aren't any. It's a bit like we still use the word 'broadcasting' to describe sending a radio signal from transmitter to receiver. But the word doesn't distinguish between the ordinary and the extraordinary. It could mean anything from a crude walkie-talkie with a range of 10 metres to a satellite 24,000 miles above our heads transmitting a high definition, three dimensional, colour television picture to a 70 inch LED flat screen TV.

Any of the following words could justifiably be used in connection with some aspects of dowsing...mysterious, supernatural, paranormal, mystical, psychic, clairvoyant, uncanny, bizarre, mumbo-jumbo, weird. Dowsing creates a bridge between two worlds – those of the visible and the invisible.

In computer terms, by the time we have finished you will be using your dowsing as a kind of spiritual search engine – an extra-dimensional Google searching all that is known for answers to anything and everything: From, 'Will this melon be ripe in time for my dinner party on Wednesday?' To, 'How many past lives have I lived?' From, 'Should I wear a waterproof coat today?' To, 'Why is my relationship not working?' You can dowse for the answer to anything and that is our key to psychic power.

1 OUR JOURNEY BEGINS

Never has the ancient and subtle art of dowsing been more appropriate than for our 21st Century times. As I take you on a tour of dowsing, bear in mind that everything you read is going to have a relevance to the ultimate purpose of this book – to help you become a powerful psychic able to achieve your psychic ambitions and fulfill the true destiny that is meant for your life.

But to get to this destination you need fully to understand what dowsing is all about - its background, history and the practicalities of learning how to dowse. In other words, to become a good psychic you need first to be a good dowser.

Stick with it and I will guide you step by step – from the early days when you amaze yourself that dowsing works for you, all the way to using your psychic powers to make a big difference to your life and to the world around you. And you won't need to accomplish an all-round expertise in dowsing before moving on to psychic matters – the two will develop together. As you learn about dowsing we will apply it to the psychic realm. Each step you take in dowsing will be a step towards achieving your psychic potential.

First a quick summary, so you can get your head round the concept of dowsing.

What is dowsing? It is a way of gaining information not available to our five senses. It is a bridge between our intuition and the information field 'out there' usually accessed by geniuses, savants, mystics and psychics. Dowsing empowers us to access and help the world beyond the limitations of our rational mind.

Who can dowse? Pretty well everyone.

Is it easy to learn? Yes, but while most people can learn quickly to get a 'Yes' or 'No' response to their questions many fail to get the *correct* 'Yes' or 'No'. To get it right more often than by random chance takes persistence and practice. Many potentially good dowsers give up because they get discouraged by early mistakes and haven't the determination to learn from those mistakes and keep practising.

How does it work? No-one really knows and this is what makes it exciting. The best brains in the world can't explain it but thousands of examples of successful dowsing proves that dowsing is real.

What are the dowsing tools? The primary instrument is the mind of the dowser. To engage the subconscious in the dowsing process the dowser uses any of four main devices - the pendulum, the Y-rod (forked stick), the L-rod, or something called the bobber. These act as indicators much as a needle on a gauge. The tools respond giving yes/no (or true/false) answers to carefully worded questions. Dowsing is sometimes called divining which indicates that the source of the answers might be from a higher consciousness or the Universal Mind. The biggest dowsing tool of all, though, is your INTENT. We'll talk more about this later but for now all you need to know is that a human being's conscious intention can change the world. Through all the many years of researching the metaphysical, esoteric, mystical, occult, paranormal, the Unexplained, the Mysterious and Things That Go Bump in the Night I have come to the conclusion that The Mind is the one factor common to them all.

Or perhaps that should be 'consciousness.' The human consciousness is what connects with the Field, or the Zero Point Field, or the Cosmic Consciousness, or The Akashic Record or Out There or however you want to think of as the Universal Mind.

And what has this got to do with real life? Your mind's accessing the Universal Consciousness is like your computer exploring the internet...All the answers are there if you know where to look.

And how do you know where to look? The practice

of dowsing is the key.

The more the digital age dominates our lives the less we are feeling connected to the world of nature around us. The dowsing tool gives us back that connectedness with the universe in both a practical and spiritual way. On the one hand dowsing can be used for locating minerals, water, archaeological remains or lost objects; on the other it can detect unseen energies, both natural and man-made. The psychic dowser can takes this further and connect with angels, spirits, entities, previous lives, the past and the future.

The governing body of dowsing in the UK is the British Society of Dowsers. Within the organization there are four sub groupings which is a good indication of the four main areas that dowsing is used in today. They are: Water and Minerals, Archaeology, Health, and Earth Energies (now also known as Subtle Energies). A brief idea of each follows.

Despite the fact that dowsing is an incredible skill available to 99 per cent of the human population, most people only have a dim awareness of what it is. The most common conception is of an elderly gent in a tweed jacket plodding across a field waving about a forked stick while seeking underground water. This common notion is not wrong and there are many water dowsers who are engaged, even in this day and age, to look for underground streams. In fact despite the advanced technologies of the 21st Century, the dowsing skill is in more and more demand as water, globally, becomes scarcer. I believe shortage of water to satisfy the needs of a growing world population is a crisis that will dominate this century. Wars will not be fought over oil any more but over water. This is because, in October 2011, the global population passed seven billion and is currently rising by seventy million a year.

As the human race grows it competes more and more fiercely for this precious resource because whatever water is on the planet today is the same as was here a million years ago. In other words as more and more people are born there is less and less water to go round. And to make the statistics worse, of all the water on planet earth today only about 2 per cent of it is fresh, and 1.6 percent of this is locked up in the polar ice caps and glaciers. So, you may want to forget about developing your psychic powers and just learn to be a good water dowser because you're going to be in increasing demand as current supplies dry up! In fact there is a serious shortage of good water dowsers.

As I said earlier, water and mineral dowsing is one of the four main disciplines of dowsing today and is what you might call a tangible skill. If a minerals dowser says there is oil to be found under a certain terrain in the US, Norway or Saudi Arabia he or she is either going to be correct or incorrect. The fact that good dowsers are right more often than they are wrong proves that dowsing works. Legendary dowser George Applegate, now nearly ninety at the time of writing, celebrated his eightieth birthday by locating successfully his two-thousandth borehole. Author of the book The Complete Guide to Dowsing, George's advice to learner dowsers is something relevant to us in our quest for psychic power: 'Mistakes are important and helpful – as long as we learn from them. You don't learn from success, which goes to your head.'

One of George's greatest challenges was dowsing for water in Perth, Western Australia after a four year drought. There was no grass, the livestock were dying, and the situation had become dire. George found his spot and advised his client that he would have to drill down six thousand feet – a highly expensive operation. In the event they found a plentiful supply of water that was thirty thousand years old. How could one man, with only a forked stick, find something that had eluded even the most skilled geologists in the world? A sixth sense. Intuition, honed with practice, is the answer.

We all have the same intuitive abilities as George. And it is these same intuitive abilities that will connect us with the psychic realm.

2 THE FIRST STEPS

The second divining discipline that can be described as tangible is archaeological dowsing. When the archaeological dowser says there are remains of an iron-age fort, or a Roman villa, six feet under the surface of the soil he or she will be quickly proved right or wrong. For decades traditional archaeologists, qualified after years of study, were irritated by these amateur Johnny-come-latelies who would pluck, seemingly out of the air, information about what lay under the ground.

But after many examples of dowsers successfully identifying in minutes what conventional archaeology might take weeks to uncover, there is now a grudging acceptance in the profession that these 'amateurs' have something valuable to offer. For instance, dowsing can allow a wide and thorough site survey to be conducted, either on the ground or from a map, with great efficiency in both time and resources. The concealed presence of structures, of artefacts and of all manner of residue from previous habitation, or how the site was used by its community, can be ascertained by dowsing, allowing analysis to be performed in a non-intrusive manner, without the necessity of disturbing, damaging or otherwise interfering with a location. That is not to say that this has made redundant the legitimate scientific techniques like ground-penetrating radar and geophysical survey. The two approaches can work hand in hand.

In his book, Dowsing - One Man's Way, J.S. Scott Elliot lists eighteen case studies in the UK where dowsing was solely responsible for the discovery of an archaeological site, or new information, which was subsequently verified.

But, surely the archaeo-dowser is using what most people would call psychic powers? How else can you explain how he/she walks across a site with a pair of L-rods, or a pendulum, and says, 'This was a Roman Villa dating back to 60 AD...' Waving at a patch of bare earth s/he will say, 'There are the walls, there was a window here and a door over there. The path from the main door led to a lake over there. In this instance the dowser is going back in time. Yes, time travel happens. More of this later.

The two areas of dowsing that you might call intangible, and the ones that will have most relevance for us as psychics, are Health dowsing and Earth (or subtle) Energies. The following is where it starts to get really interesting for those of us who want to learn about, and master, other dimensions.

3 HEALTH AND HEALING

If you Google 'health dowsing' there are literally hundreds of sites dealing with the subject. Click through them and you will rapidly suffer from Overwhelm Syndrome. I'll try to take you painlessly through the essentials and show you how this gets us nearer to our psychic objective.

Firstly, health dowsing can range from simply checking out whether you, or a 'client', has an intolerance to a certain kind of food or drink – wheat and grain, shellfish, dairy products etc – to something far more serious like ascertaining the cause of a life-threatening disease like cancer. Some health dowsers progress naturally to the field of healing. The novice health dowser generally starts with dowsing for a possible mineral deficiency in the daily intake, or which health supplements might be beneficial, moving on to food allergies and food intolerances. The health dowser might later progress to deficiencies in a person's energy body. And here is where we seamlessly cross from the physical and tangible to what you might call the spiritual and intangible.

I believe that our invisible energy bodies are the key to our physical health – if the energy body is out of kilter this will reflect in the physical body in the form of anything from mild headaches to cancer. When health dowsers move into this territory they will be dealing with chakras, meridians and energy healing. What the sceptic might term 'mumbo-jumbo.'

We'll look later in more detail at energy healing as it could fill several books as a topic in its own right but at this stage we just want to get a feel for what dowsing's all about and how it fits into our quest for developing our psychic potential. As I said, health dowsing is where we cross from the tangible to the intangible and to the invisible world around us that we can't see, touch, feel, taste or hear but is nevertheless a major influence on our lives. There are hundreds of health dowsers practising world-wide and there is an International Association of Health Dowsers.

But if Health Dowsing has moved us into the realm of the unseen, it's the last category of dowsing mentioned earlier, Earth Energies, in which we boldly go where no-one has gone before: to the Final Frontier – the land of the X-Files! Before you think Earth Energy dowsers are a small community of woolly-hat wearing weirdos, practitioners can be numbered in their thousands and they are as normal as you and me.

So what is Earth Energy Dowsing? The short answer is it's using the dowsing tool to 'communicate with' invisible forces around us. These forces can be natural, emanating from the earth or the cosmos, or man-made like microwaves and other electromagnetic frequencies. Earth energies are probably better described as subtle energies – resonances all round us with which our bodies, minds and emotions interact all day and all night, most of the time without us realising it. These frequencies are capable of enhancing our health and well being or killing us. Dowsing is a way of detecting and then utilising these emanations, turning them to our own benefit.

These invisible resonances can also be forces encountered in the realm of the paranormal like trapped spirits, ghosts, elementals and other entities. Again, if you are sceptical about the existence of such manifestations Google something like 'spirits' or 'poltergeist' and you will find hundreds of stories of how real people, like you and me, have had their lives blighted by such phenomena. Oh, yes, they are real all right. And the psychic dowser can, and must, protect themselves against it, which we'll talk about later.

There, in brief, are the four main areas of dowsing. But, don't worry, you won't need to achieve the expertise of a George Applegate before you graduate to the psychic realm – all we need is to know and understand the basics of the dowsing art generally before moving on to use our skills to become intuitives.

4 THE PSYCHIC WORLD

The UK organization which deals with all manner of psychic matters is the Society for Psychical Research. The SPR, the first learned body of its kind, was founded in London in 1882. In their own words 'for the purpose of investigating that large body of debatable phenomena designated by such terms as mesmeric, psychical and spiritualistic, and to do so "in the same spirit of exact and unimpassioned enquiry which has enabled Science to solve so many problems."' Its early membership included a future Prime Minister of England, Arthur Balfour. Other prominent figures who became members included the physicist William Barrett, the experimental physicist Lord Rayleigh, Gerald Balfour, classical scholar and philosopher and Eleanor Sidgwick, one of the Balfour clan and wife of Henry Sidgwick. Eleanor was a mathematician and later Principal of Newnham College, Cambridge. Once again we see not cranks but people of repute, taking a serious interest in the world of the paranormal.

The SPR was the first organisation established to examine allegedly paranormal phenomena using scientific principles. Its aim is to learn more about events and abilities commonly described as 'psychic' or 'paranormal' by supporting research, sharing information and encouraging debate. Its membership is worldwide and represents a variety of academic and professional disciplines.

Its interests today include, among many other things, telepathy, dreams, hauntings, time travel, mediumship, near death experiences, after death communication, possession, reincarnation, UFOs, crop circles and discarnate beings. As we will see there are many cross-overs between dowsing and these paranormal phenomena. And the common denominator that bridges the two fields is our human consciousness. It is when we are in an 'altered state' that we encounter the psychic realm; when dowsers dowse, their minds are in an altered state. In fact the brains of some experienced diviners enter as deep a meditative condition within seconds as that attained by Buddhist monks who have taken years of dedication and discipline to learn the skill. In experiments where dowsers have been hooked up to EEG machines that measure brainwaves it's been found that the act of dowsing brings the left and right sides of the brain together in perfect harmony. This is the Holy Grail for meditators. When their Beta, Alpha, Theta and Delta brainwaves synchronise, a portal opens to other worlds.

From a scientific point of view Alpha, Theta and Delta are considered to be the 'altered states' frequencies. Children attain this condition naturally while adults are in Beta most of the time because we are preoccupied with the practicalities of life. This is why children take to dowsing so readily – they are not side-tracked and they don't analyze what's happening: they just do it!

As humans we are each amazing and have an amazing potential. Our minds have tremendous power; properly focused we have dominion over both the physical and extrasensory worlds. Scientists now accept that Quantum Physics proves we physically affect the world around us. But the quantum world is Alice in Wonderland stuff; there is no cause and effect, no time as we perceive it, and something can be in two places at the same time. But, weirdly and wonderfully, nothing can happen, or come into being, in this world, without first being brought to life by the human consciousness. Science's shorthand for this phenomena is 'the Observer Creates Reality.' In other words we are interacting all the time with the forces around us and have the power to shape our destinies if we put our minds to it – literally!

Nobody understands it, maybe, but thousands of experiments across the decades have now proven the basic tenets of the Quantum Universe - that in some mysterious way human consciousness conjures up what we see around us. Our daily existence is like pictures on a TV – it is made up of two realities. One is the picture you see in front of you and the other is the invisible frequencies carrying the picture. Access the frequencies and you change the picture – or our reality. The human consciousness is what connects with the Field, or the Zero Point Field, or the Cosmic Consciousness, or The Akashic Record or Out There or the 'Information Field' or however you want to think of as the Universal Mind.

I am going to go off at a bit of a tangent here but stick with it because it's all part of the 'matrix' which we as dowsers and psychics are a part of and the better we understand the underlying science the more able we will be to become the best at what we do. And the Quantum World is what makes it all work. If you Google 'quantum' you will find thousands of references – from the sciences of Quantum Physics and Quantum Mechanics to the art of mind/body Quantum Healing. Consider this quote from Nobel Prize winning American Physicist Richard Feynman, 'The Big Bang happened because I thought of it; I thought of it because the Big Bang happened.'

Think about this quote. Dr Feynman was talking in the context of the mysterious world of quantum mechanics which scientists now agree overturns the old, comfortable, Newtonian 'billiard ball' universe where everything operates like a clock with time moving from the past, through the present and into the future.

In the quantum world, there is no time as we perceive it, and the past is something we can interact with. And something can be in two places at the same time. If the observer really does create reality, the Big Bang would not have happened if someone hadn't thought of it.

BUT they only thought of it because it happened. This is so counter-intuitive that even the greatest minds, brains with super IQs, can't make sense of it. Hence another legendary quote from Dr Feynman, 'I think I can safely say that nobody understands quantum mechanics.'

Nobody understands it, maybe, but thousands of experiments across the decades have now proven the basic doctrine of the Quantum Universe - that in some mysterious way our human consciousness conjures up what we see around us.

For his contributions to the development of quantum electrodynamics, Richard Feynman received the Nobel Prize in Physics in 1965. If you want to read more about the intricacies of the Quantum World, and its connection with dowsing, there is more in Appendix 1. So what do we now know..? The universe is one huge consciousness and all things are part of that consciousness. Everything resonates with its own, individual frequency. Animals, vegetables and minerals have unique resonances but the universal consciousness links us all together. Our frequencies make up our energy bodies which are mirrored by the physical body which we can see. But, we are all connected through the universal consciousness - thus we can talk to stones, plants, trees and they can talk to us. All we have to do is listen.

The part of our minds that interacts with the

unseen world is our intuitive, Right Brain. Technically the human brain is divided into two halves – the left is the bossy thinker making day-to-day decisions; the right is the dreamer, in touch with higher realities. From a scientific viewpoint the mind is split into two very powerful computers. The Left Brain uses logic, deals with detail and facts rule. It handles language and mathematics and is a hard-nosed realist. The Right Brain has hunches and feelings. It looks at the big picture, loves using its imagination and can make intuitive leaps that the Left Brain can only dream of. Here's a quote that backs this up: 'The intellect has little to do on the road to discovery; there comes a leap in consciousness – call it intuition or what you will – and the solution comes to you and you don't know why or how.' The person who said that was Albert Einstein, arguably the greatest scientific genius of the 20th Century.

Our Right Brains are our unsung heroes. While the Left Brain takes all the credit for managing our lives, it's really the Right Brain that runs things. From handling the million daily functions that keep us healthy, like digesting our food, pumping our hearts and keep our glands working efficiently, it also houses our unconscious mind that runs 90 per cent of our lives. And it's this unconscious mind we need to get to know better if we are to become powerful psychics. Our unconscious is our friend and is there to help us achieve our potential. But, unwittingly, it can also be the storehouse of long-forgotten traumas and memories which have an unseen influence on our daily existence. And that is why some adults have deep-seated health issues. Such is the versatility of the psychic world that some of these issues can be healed and we'll come to more on that later in this book.

I hope we are now beginning to see a logical picture emerging, showing the link between dowsing and developing psychic potential.

5 SO JUST DO IT…

Before we go on to the practicalities of dowsing, there are some game-changers which will make all the difference between you becoming a hit-and-miss dowser and a great dowser. And, therefore, a great psychic practitioner.

First, a dowser needs clarity and focus and has to ask the right questions. It is important to attune yourself before you start to dowse, giving yourself time to get 'in the zone'. If your head is full of day-to-day niggles then you will not be in the right frame of mind. You must ask a specific question which will illicit a 'yes' or 'no' answer – not 'Which is better for me, tea or coffee?' But 'All things considered, is tea better for my complete being than coffee?' Remember, 'for results that are terrific it pays to be specific'! Here, you asked a question the answer to which is either going to tell you that tea is better for your general well being, or it's not. I can't emphasise this enough – asking the right question is fundamental to your success as a dowser. You may think this is easy to handle. All you have to do is think of the answer you need to know and the question will follow naturally. If only it was as easy as that. The annals of dowsing are riddled with examples of the enthusiastic amateur who has brought disaster down on his head by not thinking through what the right question or questions should be. Here's an example: your next-door neighbour has heard that you have these strange powers and can find underground water and he is looking for a suitable place to sink a borehole for a new source of drinking water. So he asks you if you would oblige. Flattered at his trust in you, you agree and pace up and down his large garden and, sure enough, you get a strong reaction just at the edge of his lawn where it would be perfectly practical for a drilling company to access.

'Dig here and you'll find water at thirty meters,' you confidently declare. After watching your odd antics, wandering up and down his garden holding a forked stick, he is wondering if he's done the right thing asking this strange person to do anything as scientific as locating something you can't see, or smell or hear or touch without using geological maps, underground radar and all the other paraphernalia of the professional geo/marine engineering company.

But now that he has asked he doesn't want the embarrassment of ridiculing your methods so, persuaded by your confident shrug of the shoulders, he decides to call in the drillers. A month and ten thousand pounds later the driller announces the good news that they have, indeed, found a plentiful supply of water. However, the bad news is that it's too salty to drink!

That is because when you were searching for a source of underground water you did not ask for DRINKABLE water. By not asking the correct question you, the dowser, have cost your neighbour half his savings and he will probably never talk to you again. Oh dear! Remember, the 'information field' out there is just like a computer – rubbish in and rubbish out. It cannot interpret what you meant to ask – it just answers the question.

Apart from not asking the right question, there are other impediments to successful dowsing. These include dehydration, poor health and something called 'reversed polarity.' So make sure you have drunk enough water before dowsing, and that you feel well. Reversed polarity happens to us all and it changes our 'yes' to a 'no' and vice-versa (very confusing). You can check if this is the case by asking your pendulum a question you know the answer to – 'Was I born in Brighton?' for instance. If you get the wrong answer then you probably have reversed polarity. To change back, thump the top of your chest, just above the breast-bone, three times and cough at the same time. This is known as the 'Thymus thump.' I don't know how, but this method works and you can check if you are back to your old self by asking another question. By the way, don't forget to detach yourself from the answer – otherwise your ego will decide the answer it wants and that will be what you get.

Another impediment to successful dowsing is lack of

persistence, which leads to loss of confidence. Many potentially successful dowsers give up because they are not prepared to put in the time to practise. If you were learning the piano, would you expect to be able to play a Beethoven sonata after a couple of lessons? Or even bash out a singalong tune on the pub piano? Of course you wouldn't. So why should a dowser expect instant success without practice?

The final impediment is being too analytical. Don't fall into that well-known trap – 'paralysis by analysis.' The material world in which we live today has sharpened our analytical senses. But put that aside when dowsing and have faith. Stop thinking about the mechanics of it. No, you can't explain it but it still works! That's why children are so good at dowsing – they don't question it, they just do it.

So, having looked at the game-changers and the impediments, here are some more facts of dowsing life:

No dowsing is always 100% accurate – that pianist mentioned earlier will have off days; that paradigm of dowsing excellence, George Applegate, got it wrong once costing his clients £7 million when the drill bit hit a layer of rock that turned out to be impenetrable. Ooops!

As I said, pretty well anyone can dowse but it takes practice to dowse accurately – good dowsers are not born, they are made; there is no single, 'correct' way to dowse – choose the method you are most comfortable with.

If you fail and fail and fail – don't give up. It's the

'cosmic joker' who knows you have the potential to be a really good dowser and feels threatened so he will sap your confidence at every opportunity.

Let's now look at some of the practicalities of dowsing to get you started with a firm understanding of the principles and practice. Remember, there are four dowsing tools from which we can choose in order to get started – the pendulum, the L-rod, the Y-rod (forked stick) and the bobber. Most people find it convenient to start with a pendulum or L-rod so let's begin there. There is no need to spend any money to own either – you can easily make both with items you would find around the house. A pendulum is any weight suspended on a cord or thread. It could be a metal nut on a piece of string, a ring on some cotton thread or an angler's lead weight on a length of gut. As long as it hangs evenly and swings comfortably it will do.

A pair of L-rods can be fashioned out of a coat-hanger. With a pair of pliers cut both sides of the 'neck' below the twist. Straighten out the wire and cut in two. Then bend one end of each at a right angle creating a 'handle' to fit into your fist. The end result should be an L-shaped piece of wire with the shorter bit you can hold and the longer length acting as the dowsing 'antenna.'

An expensive dowsing tool will not get better results. But if you prefer to purchase a professionally-made one then the shop on the website of the British Society of Dowsers has plenty to choose from at www. britishdowsers.org.

If you get the chance to join a local dowsing group, or attend an 'Introduction to Dowsing' workshop, you will be able to learn how to use your dowsing tools in a couple of hours. But if you prefer to go it alone, it's perfectly OK. I taught myself to dowse with rods and a pendulum and then a year or so later I set up my own dowsing group which clocked up a membership of 60 within a year. If I can learn to dowse anyone can.

Back to the L-rods. You are in the privacy of your kitchen where you are looking at a bit of vandalized coat-hanger, with kinks in it where the pliers didn't quite manage to straighten it properly, and you are thinking to yourself, 'What on earth am I playing at? How can an ex-coat-hanger possibly be my portal to other dimensions? I must be mad.'

We experienced dowsers have all been through this self doubt. It's our Left Brain trying to intimidate its submissive partner the Right Brain and stop the magic in its tracks. And it's being aided and abetted by someone we're going to meet on a regular basis on our journey – the aforementioned Cosmic Joker. I'll tell you about him later but at this stage I don't want to get side-tracked. Let's carry on with learning how to use one of the most popular dowsing devices – the L-rod.

So, there you are thinking how bizarre it is that you, a normally sensible, down to earth person, are staring at two bits of bent wire which are going to help you find a portal to other worlds. 'This whole thing's a crackpot situation,' you'll be thinking. Maybe it is, but nothing ventured...So, now you've got this far pick up those rods, get the feel of them. Hold them in your fists and point them as a Wyatt Earp might in the Gunfight at the OK Corral. Don't hold them too tight. The idea is that your rods should be able to swing inwards to cross over each other, or out to form a line. Before you start walking forward keep them almost parallel with the ground except have their noses slightly dipped – slightly because if you point them too far towards the ground gravity will ensure they won't swing and if you raise them higher than level they'll flop about. A bit of practice just holding the rods and walking at the same time is the best thing to do before trying to 'find' something.

Once you're comfortable with this you can now start the important business of building a rapport with your dowsing tool. And this is one of the essentials of successful dowsing. You have to establish a mental bond between you and the rods (or pendulum or Y-rod or bobber). It's a bit like driving a car. When you first started learning you consciously went step by step through the practicalities...make sure the gearstick's in neutral, switch on the engine, depress the clutch, select first gear, check your mirrors, hands on the steering wheel, let out the clutch, press the accelerator, ease into the traffic flow when it's safe to do so...etc. Everything is a mental effort, your Left Brain is working overtime. But within a short time, as you gain experience, your good old Right Brain takes over and everything is automatic. It's almost as if you and the car are one being. Well, it's the same with dowsing.

Once you are at one with your dowsing tool your unconscious, intuition, is free to work and the rods will act as an indicator, like the needle on a guage. It will tell you, 'It's here; you've found it,' or 'Yes' or 'No' or 'True' or 'False'.

I've heard it said by some dowsers that when they started they treated their dowsing tool as you might an untrained puppy. You tell it how you want it to behave and eventually it gets the message and sits when it's told, lies down, brings you the paper etc (the dog, not the dowsing rods). All this is just an easy to understand way of making sense of something that's a bit weird. But it's an important part of the process of developing from Learner dowser to Experienced Practitioner – you start by shrugging off the sabotaging self-ridicule, pick up the rods, practise your moves step by step, establish a firm but fair master-servant relationship with your rods and allow your Left Brain to go off and do something else that it feels is more important.

After you are confident that you are 'at one' with your dowsing tool try locating something real. Hold them in what is known as 'the search position' – that is straight forward, parallel to each other. Say you are looking for where your main drain is in the yard. You walk slowly forward focusing your mind on pipework under the ground. You have a clear picture of it in your mind's eye. When you cross over the 'target' your rods should cross. If you continue to walk forwards they should uncross.

If you don't want to go outside in case your

neighbours see you and ask awkward questions you're not quite ready to answer yet, you can set up a dowsing exercise in your house. Lay down a piece of rope, or string, across the room and tell your rods to 'Show me the rope.' Walk slowly forwards repeating this as a kind of mantra, 'Show me the rope...show me the rope...' If you are extraordinarily lucky the rods will cross when you reach the rope. A tingle will go down your spine and your jaw will drop. The rods definitely moved of their own accord, you will say to yourself. And you will be hooked. Dowsing has found another follower.

But, it is more likely that nothing will happen. Try crossing the rope from the other direction, keep a picture of it in your mind (you'd forgotten to do this hadn't you?), and keep repeating the mantra, 'Show me the rope.' Like learning to drive, you are probably over-anxious about doing it right. Are the rods parallel? Am I holding them too tight? Am I walking too fast? This is the Left Brain barging your friend the Right Brain out of the way and taking over. Be patient. Keep trying. Relax. Eventually, the Left Brain will get bored and go off for a well-earned rest and your Right Brain will slip into the driving seat. Then one of the rods might twitch and move slightly. Was it my imagination? Try again. This time the twitch might become a bit of a swivel. Congratulations! Your rods have got the message. Keep practising. And rest a bit in between sessions. And drink plenty of water. This is another dowsing essential. As I explained earlier, there are a number of impediments to dowsing and one of them is being dehydrated. If your body needs water it will not be able to dowse properly.

Oh yes, it's your body doing the dowsing not your rods. It's called the ideomotor effect –something inside us reacts and causes the dowsing tool to move in a certain way. Remember, the tool is just an indicator but it boosts the confidence when it tells us the answer we're looking for. Some seasoned dowsers don't need any tools – they just dowse with their hands, or eyes or arms. But most of us need the reassurance that information is being received and communicated in a way we can perceive. With that twitch of the L-rod you have begun your journey to psychic power. With that twitch of the L-rod we experience the definition at the beginning of this book of the word 'Psychic' - 'faculties or phenomena that are apparently inexplicable by natural laws.' So the psychic in you is already awakening like some inner sleeping beauty, stretching and blinking in the light.

6 PENDULUM POWER

Probably the best known of the dowsing tools is the Pendulum – just a weight suspended by a string or thread but in some people's minds it is as magical as a wizard's wand.

How long you make the cord or chain or string is a matter of choice. But remember, the longer it is the longer the swing and the longer it takes to get an answer. I suggest you try something between four and six inches. Now here's where a lot of people get frustrated, before they have even begun. Because they dangle the pendulum, motionless, and ask their question. Nothing happens. They try again. Again, nothing happens. Confidence begins to ebb. They ask again, perhaps rephrasing the question in case the pendulum didn't understand the first one! Nothing. Frustration sets in and it's very tempting to throw the whole thing out of the window and get back to familiar things like paying the gas bill or taking the dog for a walk. The pendulum just hangs there, mocking. Don't despair. All you need to do is set the pendulum going in what's known as 'the search position.' That is, with a flick of the wrist nudge the pendulum into a diagonal swing so that it has some energy behind it.

Gradually the back and forth diagonal will transform into a uniform clockwise or anti- clockwise movement. At this point I should say that you need to establish your own, unique 'yes' and 'no' signal. For many people clockwise means 'yes' and anti-clockwise is a 'no.' But for some it's the opposite. For others a 'yes' is an up and down motion like a head nodding, with swinging to the left and right, like a head shaking, meaning 'no.' Whatever you feel comfortable with, and what works for you, is your own, unique response.

There is no right or wrong way so long as the signal is consistent – remember the danger of 'reversed polarity' mentioned earlier. A good way to check out your yeses and noes is to dangle the pendulum first over your right knee and then your left – after giving it a diagonal 'nudge' of course. As the right knee is positive and the left negative you should get a 'yes' movement and then a 'no.' There is a third reaction which you should be aware of – and that's a confused swinging and circling that makes no sense to you. This is your pendulum's way of saying, 'That's a daft question – how can I answer that correctly?' For instance, 'Am I a good person?' Good in what way? Good for a laugh? Good to animals? Good for a cannibal to eat? Don't forget, in asking your question you are dialoguing with the Eternal Information Matrix which knows everything. However, much like a computer, it takes things literally.

Unlike you or me it cannot judge the nuances, or the tone of voice. Or whether you are being ironic. It will answer you literally.   When it comes to a debatable question it won't answer at all.   That is why it is so important to be precise in your questioning. It's is no good asking your pendulum 'Is there water under this field?' It will probably tell you 'yes'. But while you meant 'drinkable' water, it's just telling you that there's water, which turns out to be sewage. Remember, 'For results that are terrific it pays to be specific.' If you were a water dowser asking that last question of his forked stick you would probably say something like, 'Show me drinkable water, flowing all year round, at a rate of at least 200 litres a minute, at less than 30 metres in depth.' Long-winded, yes, but the rods are left in no doubt about the answer you are seeking.

7 ASK WITH A 'Y'

With the 'Y' rod we're back to the tweed-jacketed gent plodding across a field looking for underground water. This is the image that most non-dowsers recognize and think is what dowsing's all about. Isn't dowsing something to do with finding water? They ask. In the old days our gent used a forked branch, usually hazel, and trimmed to size. These days the Y-rod is more hi-tech and is manufactured from plastic or polyamide or any sort of springy metal. You hold the Y-rod between both thumbs and wrap your hands around handle end, turning your wrists upwards to create a tension with the device which then quivers like a greyhound in the traps.

Once you have the grip right, walk forward asking to be shown underground water. When you cross a stream the rod will either jerk upwards or down. Either way, it's as well to be prepared as the end can give you a nasty wack. And, by the way, for water read also minerals, precious metals or even oil – the water dowser is just as capable of finding other tangible things hidden underground. And another wonder of the human mind is illustrated here. The dowser finds what he is looking for. So, if he (or she of course - for convenience I'm saying he but there are probably more female dowsers these days than male) is looking for gold but right next to the seam of gold ore is an underground stream, the Y-rod will ignore the water and only indicate the metal!

The last popular dowsing device is the wand or bobber. This is a flexible length of wood or plastic, thick at one end tapering to a thin point. It's the thin end that you hold with the weight of the thick end giving it its nodding motion. I usually visualize a fishing rod held by the thin end here. To make your own bobber, cut a piece of tapering hazel between three and five feet long. Cut off all protruding bits until you have a long, flexible stick. Hold it by the thin end and walk forward. It will bob up and down and this is your search position. As you connect with your target the end will behave like the pendulum only this time its 'yes' or 'no' will be denoted by a vertical or horizontal ellipse. Again, if you don't want to make one yourself they can be purchased manufactured from plastic, copper or stainless steel.

Well that's quick gallop through the kind of tools dowsers use. For the purposes of learning the essentials of connecting your intuition to the Information Field we'll stick to the L-rod or pendulum from now on. And one final essential: most serious dowsers believe they are communing with an intelligence outside themselves when they dowse. Consequently, they approach their dowsing with a sense of respect. They demonstrate this by always asking permission before dowsing. It's a very simple process but one that's good to get into the habit of adopting. Before dowsing, ask the three questions Can I...? May I...? Should I...? Can I means have I the ability in this instance and am I ready? May I means do I have your (the outside intelligence) permission? And should I means is it appropriate and proper to dowse this questions here and now? If you get a 'No' to any of these questions, postpone the exercise until later.

8 TALKING WITH OTHER DIMENSIONS

The first thing the dowsing and psychic worlds have in common is the need for the practitioner's mind to be in an 'altered state.' This is an indispensable condition if you want to be a good dowser or psychic. And what exactly is an altered state? It's where the busy left brain, the one that deals with everyday practicalities, is quietened down allowing the submissive right brain to get into the driving seat. This happens automatically in certain circumstances - for example, when experienced dowsers are seeking their target, or asking their pendulum whether the answer is 'yes' or 'no' or 'maybe'. Or it's when the medium sinks into a trance to allow the spirit world to speak through him/her. Or when we are in bed in the twilight world between being awake and asleep. Or it's like when you are driving a car and find when you have reached your destination you can't remember anything of the route you've just taken. Or when Albert Einstein is daydreaming about what energy is and

E=mc2 pops into his head.

Getting yourself into an altered state is easier said than done. Yes, it happens automatically once you are driving along a familiar road but to get into an altered state to order takes practice and persistence. The more you practice, the quicker it happens – as I said, experienced dowsers will enter such a state instantly as they lock their mind onto the objective. Or a medium will make the transition within seconds. Dowsers and those who want to progress in psychic matters must know how to get rapidly into this Alpha brainwave state. The human brain has four ranges of frequencies it works with, depending on the job it's doing – Beta. Alpha, Theta and Delta. Alpha is our friend and the state we want to fall into every time we want to dowse or do psychic things. Adding Theta and Delta is even better but Alpha will give us all we need.

Beta, between 13-40Hz, is what we use for alertness, concentration, making decisions.

Alpha, 7-13Hz is for relaxation, visualization and creativity and what we need for accessing the great computer in the sky. Theta, 4-7Hz, is for meditation, intuition, memory and can also be useful to us for linking our subconscious to what's 'out there.' Delta, 0-4Hz, is for healing and deep sleep.

How do we get into that ideal Alpha state? There are many ways to access this meditative mode – and the more you practice, the easier it becomes. Like dowsing, there is no single right way – what works for me might leave you frustratedly in Left Brain mode thinking of all the shopping you've got to do to cater for guests coming at the weekend. But you could try something like this: Sit or lie comfortably and gently relax your eyelids and softly close them. Now roll your eyes up 20 degrees in your head as if you were looking at your eyebrows - this happens naturally when you transition into your normal sleeping state, so you will immediately begin to relax. Breathe comfortably and slowly, and focus on your breathing. Begin counting backwards from 50 down to zero. Pace yourself at one numeral per second. When you arrive at 5 stop and mentally tell yourself that you will be totally relaxed and in the Alpha state when you reach zero. Start the countdown again and, again, stop – this time at 3 telling yourself the same thing. Then finish the countdown to zero and enjoy going into Alpha easily and effortlessly, in only a few short seconds. Keep your eyes closed and pretend you are looking at a blank screen just beyond your eyebrows. At first you will see very little – perhaps lots of dots, or swirling coloured whisps. Nothing coherent. But, gradually, elusive forms will become more recognisable. They could form into a face, or a scene, or an animal. Personally, I pay attention to these pictures as they bubble into my mind, I notice how they develop, then I mentally step inside the scene.

Basically, getting into Alpha mode is like day dreaming – you switch off the active side of your mind and just drift into a world of your own. For a more detailed look at a range of methods of attaining an altered state see

Appendix 3.

The material world around us that we can see and touch and with which we relate, is just the visible surface of a seething flux of energies which govern our lives. We can't see them but we interact, consciously or unconsciously, every moment of our earthly lives. These unseen swirlings can perform feats which are undeniable but which no-one can explain.

Getting in touch with these energies by using mind-altering substances is not to be recommended. In fact, it would be irresponsible and dangerous for a dowser or psychic to do this as the results would not be accurate or helpful. Another reason to steer clear of this temptation is that using drugs opens portals from the human mind to other dimensions inhabited by spirit 'chancers' who will eagerly latch onto you while your defences are down. They include spirits of humans who no longer have a carnate body, demonic entities who take over your mind and body for their own purposes, and even floating, nomad consciousnesses (some believe they are ETs) who lodge themselves in the life force of living humans.

Why doesn't this happen when a dowser or psychic enters an altered state? Because, so long as they remain 'in control' of their minds, their defences are strong and entities and attachments don't have the power. It's only when humans weaken their defences by voluntarily imbibing excessive quantities of alcohol, or take narcotics, or become mentally weak for other reasons that discarnate energies invade.

So the first action we take before dowsing or entering the psychic realm is to protect ourselves. So long as live human beings are in command of their senses they have dominion over all entities from other dimensions. However, these entities will certainly try bluffing you into being afraid and lowering your guard but they have no real power to harm, unless you invite them into your life for whatever reason (more details on this later). But, to be doubly sure, it's as well to take simple precautions. There are lots of ways to do this but the principle is to call on the highest power for good in the universe to provide you with a protective shield of white or golden light. Imagine yourself floating in a bubble, or cocoon, of brilliant light through which no harmful energies can enter. Some dowsers or psychic workers call this protective shield to encase them just prior to working with other dimensions. But it's not a bad idea to make this part of your daily routine. When you get up in the morning – or while you're still lying in bed – imagine this light bubble descending to envelope you in a warm, protective, womb-like security. You can say something like, 'I am surrounding myself with a wonderful bubble of white light which will protect me from all detrimental energies, from any time, any place, any dimension, any frequency, any reality. No harmful energy can penetrate my shield but it will allow all beneficial energies to get through to me and flow out from me.'

Some people like to imagine a mirror-like coating on the outside of their cocoon which reflects back into the light all harmful energies – spirit attachments, entities, ETs, curses, thought forms, human negativity and anything else detrimental.

And this brings me neatly on to giving you more information on just what these harmful energies might be. What form they take. And shortly we will be conducting our first experiment using our early dowsing skills to detect if we have any of these entities near us. But before that, a bit more essential information. We are actually surrounded by all kinds of invisible entities who inhabit dimensions right next door to ours. In fact they can even occupy the same space as us but, because they are on a different frequency, we are not aware of them in our day-to-day lives. This is all very counter-intuitive and even if you are willing to be persuaded about all this the good old logical left brain keeps throwing up objections.

The way I try to explain it to myself is by thinking of a parallel situation which my left brain is comfortable with: Entities all around us that we can't see? Come on, do you really expect me to believe that? Says my know-all rational mind. Well, how about radio waves? You don't see those, or feel them, but turn on a wireless and tune to the right frequency...and there's a news report, or music or a discussion coming out of the speaker. Without the radio we cannot detect these frequencies (although I did once hear of someone who was picking up radio transmissions through the fillings in their teeth, but that's another story). In principle, entities are the same as those radio waves – they exist as frequencies which operate on different levels from our own. If you think of the electromagnetic spectrum for a minute (this is the range of frequencies that scientists agree on). It stretches from below the very low frequencies used for modern radio communication to gamma radiation at the short-wavelength (high-frequency) end, thereby covering wavelengths from thousands of kilometers down to a fraction of the size of an atom. The limit for long wavelengths is the size of the universe itself, while it is thought that the short wavelength limit is in the vicinity of the Planck length squared although in principle the spectrum is infinite and continuous. There are many types of entities and I'll list a few in a minute, but I like to think of them as discrete forms of consciousness existing in the ether all round us; they have their own roles in the Great Scheme Of Things and sometimes they interact with us. They seem to have the ability to adjust their frequencies to ours, while we find it much harder to do it the other way round. When other entities impinge on our world we sometimes know about it but mostly we are completely unaware. Psychically, it's a jungle out there! Please don't get the impression that every invisible force is a threat to us humans. Some are but there are many who are helpful and who protect us. Just like here on this earthly plane, there are good people and bad people in the realms beyond this one. Here are some of the types which move in and out of our world (but this list is by no means exhaustive): Apparitions, ghosts, phantoms, poltergeists, doppelgangers, trapped spirits, demonic entities, ETs, angels, elementals like fairies, elves, devas, leprechauns etc., animals spirits, succubus, incubus and so on. Let's have a look at some of these in more detail.

Apparitions: It's another word for a ghost or other supernatural entity. They can be of humans, animals or inanimate objects, such as houses, or of non-human entities. Apparitions can be of both the living and the dead. Because they exist on a different frequency from our material plane they can pass through solid objects.

Ghosts: The most 'common' variety of spiritual entities, ghosts are simply humans who have lived in the past and have experienced a terrifying ordeal, or suffered some kind of extreme trauma. The resulting emotional turmoil has imprinted itself on its surroundings and 'replays' the events when the human observer is on the same wavelength. A ghost does not interact with its observers but seems stuck on a loop, repeating endlessly the scene which could have happened hundreds of years previously.

Phantom: Another word for ghost, apparition or spectre but is often the preferred definition of mass sightings like that of a phantom army still fighting a battle in the English Civil War. Again, witnesses report seeing, and sometimes hearing, ghostly combat but there is never any interaction with the observers.

Poltergeist: The German word for noisy ghost and these definitely do interact with humans. The increasingly accepted theory is that an invisible presence in a household draws energy from one of the family to carry out a reign of terror. Pots and pans are thrown around, graffiti is scrawled on the walls, mysterious pools of water appear on the floor and furniture moves about of its own accord. Rarely are its human victims actually harmed physically but mentally they are often traumatized.

Doppelganger. Again a German word meaning double walker. This is the appearance of a 'double,' or an apparition of a living person. Doppelgangers may act as ominous warnings of impending tragedy. Abraham Lincoln is famously said to have witnessed his own doppelganger, before he was assassinated. Some psychic investigators believe a doppelganger is a projection of human consciousness that somehow takes on a recognizable form.

Spirits: These are the essences of a once living human being that, for whatever reason, have not moved on to the next stage of their eternal destiny. Spirits that fail to make a full transition to the next level can become stuck or 'earthbound'. These life forms can then either latch on to a living person, an individual, or to a place such as a home or workplace. Incidentally, some dowsers make a speciality of helping these 'trapped souls.' Having detected them, dowsers offer to lead them to the light giving them that last important nudge to continue fulfilling their individual destinies. Some say this is one of the most benevolent services a human can offer in this life.

Demonic entities: Demons are manifestations of an evil consciousness that has never lived as a human being. They usually appear in people's lives after having been 'invited.' The most common way for a demonic entity to get a toehold on this plane is via seemingly innocent games involving divination – using a ouija board for instance. Playing around asking, 'Is anybody there' is a highly dangerous activity which opens a portal for any evil Tom, Dick or Harry to walk in. And they are queueing up just waiting for the opportunity. As there is no such thing on 'the other side' as time, these chancers are happy to hang around, for eternity if necessary, just to get the right signal. When they do, they latch on and their victim is in for a very rough ride.

Angels: These are the good guys of the psychic world. They are immortal, supernatural beings there to help us – all we have to do is ask. They are aware of our personal life goals and are assigned to help us, but never interfere with our free will. According to dowser Jean Slatter there are thousands of unemployed angels itching to help us with whatever we need, so long as it's for the highest good. In fact Jean wrote a popular book about it called Hiring the Heavens.

ETs: Unidentified Flying Objects are the popular conception of how aliens from other planets visit Earth. But, extraterrestrials may be all around (and sometimes in) us. They could be consciousnesses like thoughts which appear to drop into our heads and lead us to take certain action. Have you ever asked yourself where thoughts come from? There are some who are convinced that thoughts are intelligent entities that 'possess' the human form and use us to carry out their purpose. When you decide to go shopping, or stay at home, or do some deadheading in the garden, is it 'you' having these thoughts or is it your possessing entity that is pulling your strings for its own ends? In fact who ARE you? Are you your body? Your mind? Is there just one version of you? There are theories that most of us are inhabited by several thought entities who are often at war within us, changing our personalities as we react to events. When Mozart said 'Tunes just walk into my head' he was right. His mind was a receptacle for music dropping from the spheres. Thoughts are no different. Mozart was a genius because his thoughts were geniuses. Some of us are idiots because that's the way our thoughts are.

So, is 'out there' a jungle of competing thoughts swirling around in their own dimension, occasioinally bursting through into ours seeking a life within the vehicle of our bodies? When our bodies die do our thoughts, who inhabited us, merely re-enter their own dimension and wait for another suitable vehicle within which to continue their existence?

As I said, an interpretation of these thoughts is that they are the consciousness of ETs some of which like inhabiting a human body to experience life on a physical plane. Some are researching what life is like being a human, some are just passing through, like psychic tourists, and eventually go on their way. Some seem to arrive in our dimension in so-called UFOs but these 'craft' are manifestations of collective consciousness and are real in their own dimension but flit in and out of our reality. Alien 'abductions' are where ETs change their frequencies to match those of a human being's astral body.

Elementals: These are spirits that embody one of the five elements - Earth (solid), Water (liquid), Wind (gas), Fire (heat), Aether (quintessence). They have various popular names like fairies, elves, devas, leprechauns, gnomes, sprites, goblins, dryads and trolls. Elemental spirits possess supernatural powers and are usually invisible to humans, living in trees, rivers, plants, bogs, mountains and minerals.

Then there are bad energies of all kinds that hang around our living spaces. This phenomena is given the generic term Geopathic Stress and can be caused by a range of emanations from human thought forms, collective consciousness and curses to natural earth radiations and electromagnetic frequencies. The known effects of GS include emotional problems, marriage breakdown, hyperactive children, sleep deprivation, memory loss, mood swings, allergies and a range of physical illnesses, including life-threatening ones like MS and cancer.

Besides the detrimental environment that can be caused by Geopathic Stress, there are other 'bad energies' that can infect our space and therefore us. As we have already noted these can include poltergeists for instance – those noisy infestations that move the furniture about or make objects disappear, people float in mid-air, solid things pass through walls and other impossible things. How does this energy manifest itself? How does it perform seemingly impossible feats? And what is the intelligence behind it?

Experts now believe that this 'something' sucks the energies from human beings and uses it for its own purposes.

But these 'bad energies' need not be as dramatic as a poltergeist. They can be negative thought forms from you or anyone else who has been in your home or office. Or they can be negative emotions imprinted on one location which just hang around infecting people's moods or demeanour. They can be traumatised or displaced spirits or non-human entities or energy from curses or psychic attack. All these energies hang around making life difficult in one way or another. So, they need to be cleared out and the remaining environment rebalanced and cleansed.

9 YOU PICKED IT UP AT THE SUPERMARKET BUT YOU DID NOT BUY IT

By now you will know that we humans live in a world of energy – yes, plug in the kettle and it will use a form of energy (electricity) to transfer another kind of energy (water) into a different form of energy – steam. That chair you're sitting on is a form of energy, you are a form of energy, so are your thoughts. Energy can be solid things which, scientists say, are made of particles, or waves which are just invisible frequencies. After a titanic struggle in the scientific community early in the 19th Century (see appendix 1) it was reluctantly accepted that solid things are BOTH particles and waves. You and I are particles and waves. Whatever affects our wave bodies is reflected in our solid, particle selves.

This solidity of things – you can rap your knuckles on the table and your hand won't go through it – is only evident in this world. In other dimensions – and physicists now say that according to String Theory there must be at least 11 of them – waves rule supreme. For most of the time these dimensions are kept apart and one doesn't interfere with another. But, in certain circumstances, the energies in these other realms 'escape' into ours and that's what has caused so-called paranormal phenomena across the centuries.

Why am I telling you this? Because, as a dowser you are already crossing those boundaries. Mostly, it is to our benefit when we do. But there are dangers and that is why we talked earlier about the need for protection. I'm now going to talk about a psychic area which needs a cautious approach – Spirit Attachment.

While the limitations of our five senses confine us to perceiving that which is 'solid' around us - tables and chairs, people, mountains, trees, elephants, castles etc - we are in the midst of a pulsating universe of invisible life that sometimes spills over into our world and interacts with it.

We can use our dowsing skills to reach into that invisible realm. But, this is not something to be done casually because there are dangers lurking in the form of another brand of energy – the above-mentioned discarnate entity. In this connection most people would now think of a medium, who would go into a trance and ask: 'Is there anybody there?' We dowsers don't need a medium when we have our L-rod and pendulum.

Whenever I suspect there is an invisible presence near me I use my pendulum to ask: Is there a conscious entity of any description in my living space here and now? If I get a 'yes' answer I then dowse a list of possibilities until I narrow it down to one. My list goes something like this: Is it the spirit of a once living human being? A Ghost? Poltergeist? Is it an Elemental? Demonic entity? An ET? These are typical images that most people think of when talking about 'entities.' But your pendulum might include other categories like mass consciousness, thought forms, curses, or negative energy. This is because human beings are creating these all the time, mostly without realizing it. But these negative thoughts, once created, take on their own consciousness and are able to exist independently. For instance, a curse will see its job as destroying its target and will work to bring this about. A negative thought form is non-specific and just hangs around putting a damper on things. Mass consciousness is more general – in a war zone, for instance, the mass consciousness from both sides fight it out in their own invisible realm for supremacy. Clouds of mass consciousness descend on a location affecting the whole atmosphere of the entire community.

Because the cosmos exists in perfect balance, for every detrimental energy there's a beneficial one, so the same is happening with good vibrations which are created in the same way – when we think positively and have an optimistic outlook, our thought forms work for good. Negative entities are counter-balanced by the good guys like archangels, angels, spirit helpers and Beings of Light.

You'll see from all this that we are living in a fug of different frequencies, both good and bad. Having dowsed that you have an entity, or entities, in your home, what then? I usually take one L-rod and, holding it in the search position, gradually turn in a circle while telling the rod, 'lead me to the entity.' If you do this you will find the rod 'sticks' pointing in one direction. When it does, swivel the other way to see if it remains pointing in the same direction. Then, walk slowly forward allowing the rod to show you the way. It may take you into the hall, point up the stairs, then across the landing, to the master bedroom. As you walk through the door, it might swivel in the direction of the wardrobe and then move as it would if you were holding both rods and it was crossing with its partner. This, then, is the location of your entity. Next, use your pendulum to find out what kind of entity it is – an attachment, a demonic being or an ET consciousness. How did it get there? Let's assume that it's a spirit attachment, which means that you, or someone else in the family, brought it home with you from the supermarket run, the gym, a football match, a dinner party, or somewhere else where the invisible entity recognized you as having just the kind of frequency of energy it needs. Some attached entities may be merely curious and not have any malevolent intent at all, not realizing it could be causing you problems. Others may be more aggressive, motivated by strong desires or addictions and malevolent ones may intentionally sabotage and undermine the mental and physical health of the host to keep them in a weakened and vulnerable state.

Undetected, it would be left to wreak havoc with your moods, your energy levels would be permanently low and, depending if the attachment is particularly malicious, you could become ill, have a run of bad luck and generally lose your zest for life. A scary prospect, but there are ways you can protect yourself and tell the attachment where to get off. If it was you who brought it home just ask yourself if you have been behaving normally recently. Symptoms of a spirit attachment include low energy levels, mood swings including bouts of anger or sadness, a taunting inner voice, not feeling yourself, acting out of character, addiction to alcohol or drugs, poor memory, anxiety or depression, sudden physical problems or pain with no obvious cause, panic attacks, nightmares and a feeling of being watched.

Entities usually latch on to someone who's vulnerable in some way, which has opened a portal to their inner selves. This vulnerability could have been caused by stress, severe tiredness, grief, fear, guilt, addictions to drugs or alcohol, physical or psychological abuse or sexual abuse. Some people unwittingly, but voluntarily, open themselves up to attachments by practices like using ouija boards, or mediumship. Entities love a kindred spirit so an attachment who might have had a drinking problem while on this earth, will hang around bars and attach themselves to those who also like to drink to excess. Those who had an eating problem might latch on to someone who likes to eat a lot. The stronger the addiction, the more likely you will attract an addicted attaching entity.

Now that you have discovered an unwanted lodger,

what can you do about it? The good news is that we living humans have dominion over all such manifestations. In contrast to the popular myth perpetuated by films like The Exorcist, we aren't obliged to engage in a mortal struggle for our soul with a fiery-eyed demon. These days it's felt that a more constructive approach is far more effective. Removing attachments and leading them to the light should be a compassionate exercise, not an adversarial one. Respect, sympathy, understanding and a desire to help the entity achieve its eternal purpose is more likely to result in a satisfactory outcome for both parties. It's true, soft words do turn away wrath. So talk to it. Tell it that it should not be making your life difficult. It's in your home and it is causing you problems. 'You do not belong here,' you tell the attachment, 'So please go to the light.' In your own mind imagine a staircase in a dark room leading upwards to an open door beyond which the sky is lit with the brilliance of several suns. Ask your intruder to climb the stairs and walk into the light where he or she will find former loved ones, or people they know, waiting to take them on to the next level of their existence so that they can continue on the path that leads to their ultimate destiny. Sometimes, just occasionally, the entity will not go. He may be afraid of some imagined retribution or he may simply be quite content with his discarnate existence living off the energies of others. In which case, bless all parts of his being – emotionally, mentally and spiritually with love and take him to the door of your house, open it and ask him to leave.

But what if your unwanted visitor is a more difficult

customer like a demonic entity or an ET consciousness? How do you deal with these? So long as you have taken sensible precautions to protect yourself then the principle is the same as with attachments. But, here, you can use your pendulum or bobber. Remember, the pendulum or other dowsing tool, magnifies the power of your intent. You address the demonic energy, or the ET consciousness, and tell them to leave the person or location they have been plaguing, and progress to the next phase of their true destiny. You re-inforce your demand by swinging the pendulum or bobber anti-clockwise which has the effect of drawing the entity away from its lair. While you are doing this you call on an Angel of Light to escort it/them on their journey. At this point reverse the swing of your dowsing tool so that its force becomes positive, pushing the Dark Force into the care of the Angel of Light. Keep the clockwise movement going until you feel a sense of release which is the indication that the demon has gone. This sounds like dangerous stuff but you are quite safe so long as you have fully protected yourself. There are some simple guidelines to ensure we stay out of the clutches of these nether-world beings. Firstly, attachments are less likely to be attracted to strong, self-confident, optimistic people. Think of it like this. If you were an entity looking for an enjoyable, free ride, would you want to battle every day to stay on board? No, you want an easy time of it, so you'd plump for a weak personality who's easy to control. But we dowsers add another layer of protection – we surround ourselves with a protective white light through which no detrimental energy from any dimension or any time, past present or future, can penetrate. Think of it as a bubble, or cocoon, an impenetrable shield which is protecting you while awake and asleep. Those on board the Starship Enterprise would have called it a 'Force Field.' A reminder: You can create this Force Field with your intent. In a moment of quiet you just imagine a bubble of brilliant light all round you. Some who find it difficult to visualize might think of it as a cloak which they zip up at the front and back. Those for whom making pictures in the mind comes easy might think of a light pouring from the heavens and entering the crown chakra in the top of their heads. And then a similar beam coming up from the earth funneling into the base chakra. The two beams meet in the middle of the body and then start to expand, filling every part of the inside of the body spreading out through the skin and still expanding. As it does so it pushes before it all seven layers of the auric field, whose colors are red, orange, yellow, green, blue, indigo and violet. At the end of this visualisation process the meditator is encased in an impenetrable armour of light which would frustrate forced entry by even Beelzebub himself!

If psychic work becomes a part of your life and not just a hobby it's advisable to do a daily Grounding and Protection Exercise. Ask that power outside yourself – God, your Higher Self, the Information Field, the Matrix or however you conceive it to be, to cloak you with a protective light. If you prefer the reassurance of a detailed ritual, and you have the time, draw up the light from the earth and down from the heavens into your body and allow it to expand pushing all the colours of your being outwards to form a cocoon.

Occasionally, say once a week, you can add a cleansing ritual imagining the light moving outwards, at cellular level, through your whole body cleansing it of all detrimental energies. These would include attachments, soul fragments, all lower life forms, their seeds and tentacles, all detrimental thought forms, all parasitic energies, all cellular memories. Imagine this cleansing force spreading through your auric field cleansing it 100%. Once all this detritus is on the limits of your auric being ask for it to be taken to the light and to be converted to beneficial energy. You are now cleansed and protected from whatever the universe can throw at you. Protective cocoons aside, people who maintain a connection to the Divine, the Source, or God are vastly less vulnerable. If they hold that connection as absolute and unshakable, they are invincible.

10 GEOPATHIC STRESS

At a more down to earth level, let's look again at that umbrella term Geopathic Stress and what you, as a dowser, can do about it.

The word 'Geopathic' comes from the word geo meaning 'Earth' and 'pathos' meaning disease. It covers both naturally occurring and man-made phenomena, as well as psychic manifestations, which cause problems for us and our homes. The basic form of GS, or harmful earth energy, is radiation that rises up through the earth and is distorted by weak electromagnetic fields created by underground subterranean running water, certain mineral concentrations and geological faults. Human beings can also disturb the Earth's energies. Quarries, tunnels, mines, polluted water and railway cuttings have all been found to contribute negative effects.

With this and man-made technology, and

paranorml goings-on, adding to the resonances all around us, the original term Earth Energies have now been re-named 'subtle energies'. Together these can be:

Any geomagnetic field

Energy spirals

Water veins/underground streams

Ley lines

Energy Leys

Stress lines

Thought forms

Curses

Trapped spirits

Dark Forces

Don't forget, just because you can't see energy, doesn't mean that it isn't there!

The earth's nautural energies create straight lines through the landscape which can be beneficial, detrimental or neutral. They are of varying widths and can have several/many opposing 'bands.'

Ley lines are straight line-of-sight alignments with a minimum of five structures in a row within a five mile radius. Not all lines have a dowsable energy component.

Add to ancient energies all of man's modern transmissions and we live in an ocean of energetic 'smog.' According to the World Health Organisation '30% of all buildings are 'sick buildings. This may be caused by air quality, or by more subtle energetic pathology including earth energies and underground water.'

Well-known researchers into the effects of Earth Energies have included:

1920's - Baron Gustav Freiherr von Pohl, Germany;

1910 to 1931- Andreas Kopschina, Germany;

Early 1900's - Dr Hager, Stettin, Germany;

1933 - Dr Rambeau, Marburg, Germany;

1930's - Pierre Cody, Le Havre, France;

1970's - Kathe Bachler, Germany.

In his book Pathogens from Earth Radiations, published in 1932, Baron Von Pohl revealed that he had found that nearly every home in one street in Visbiburg, Bavaria, had someone with cancer living there. Dowsers discovered the whole street stood on a line of Geopathic Stress.

Kathe Bachler's book 'Earth Radiation' contains detailed records of the harmful effects on health that

Geopathic Stress has.

Underground water, 'stress lines,' energy leys and ley lines can cause these emanations – especially where they cross.

The biggest danger to humans is in their homes or places of work where they may remain over the negative energies for hours at a time. These detrimental energies now include radiations from microwave ovens, mobile phones, cordless phones, wi-fi and all the other electronic gizmos we take for granted.

Also, in the general mix of energies can be included Power Objects – that is objects that might have picked up negative vibrations and carry them with them. This doesn't have to be an amulet holding an ancient curse. Power objects can be innocent-seeming things like books, tables, musical instruments or jewellery.

Not all energies are unfriendly to us humans. Ley lines can be positive, too. And so can the energies found in ancient barrows, megaliths, or cathedrals.

Back to Geopathic Stress - how can it affect our health? It has often been found to be a factor in many serious long term illnesses and psychological conditions.

Research by Rolf Gordon of the Dulwich Health Society has identified that sleeping or working for long periods over a geopathic stress zone can cause sleep disturbances, headaches, anxiety and behaviour problems in children. Stronger Geopathic Stress has been linked to wasting diseases like Motor Neurone, Parkinsons and Multiple Sclerosis; also mental disorders such as addictions, suicides, depression and obsessions. And bowel disorders including IBS and Chron's disease. Other manifestations include ME, anxiety, migraines, cot death, infertility and miscarriages.

It does not necessarily mean that the Geopathic Stress *causes* these debilitating diseases, but if people have a weak constitution and are exposed to strong geopathic stress for long periods of time this can be the ultimate trigger that makes it happen.

When homes and offices are affected by the WHO's 'sick building syndrome' the people within are fractious, moody, often unwell and generally under par.

Among the best known energy lines contributing to GS are those that make up the Hartmann Grid, named after German physician, Dr Ernst Hartmann, who discovered them in 1950. The lines form a matrix around the earth, running north to south and east to west, rather like latitude and longitude lines on a map. According to Dr. Hartmann, the worst place that a person can sleep or work is over a Hartmann knot, where two Hartmann lines cross, as harmful radiation is intensified into spirals lowering the immune system causing health problems from headaches to cancer.

Even land can be stressed. Other invisible lines that

can be detrimental are Curry Lines, a similar network to the Hartmann grid but one which runs diagonally. These can be aggravated by ley lines (which connect sacred sites), earth energy lines and electro-magnetic frequencies.

Consultant physician, the late Dr Hans Nieper, claimed that 92% of all his cancer patients and 75% of his MS patients were geopathically stressed. Dr Nieper was a world-renowned cancer and MS specialist and operated one of the largest MS practices in the world, located in Germany.

The German physicist Robert Endros studied such claims with Professor KE Lotz of the School of Architecture of Biberach, West Germany. Their analysis of 400 deaths due to cancer revealed that 383 cases were related to dwellings built over geological faults, underground water veins and disturbances of the natural geomagnetic field.

The effect of GS is gradual, involving a slow deterioration in health or performance in those who are most susceptible.

Some early signs of GS are:

Disturbed sleep, waking often, on waking feeling tired;

Babies and children fret and don't sleep well;

Restlessness;

General tiredness;

'Sick building syndrome';

Chronic unwellness including ME, headaches, hyperactivity and some cancers;

A general feeling of something being not 'quite right' with a particular area or room;

Cracking or damp in a building that keeps re-occurring.

Cats seem to be immune to GS radiations and actively seek out the spots to sleep over them. Owls, snakes, high infestations of slugs and snails, insects, parasites, bacteria, viruses, ants, termites, wasps and bees all like geopathic stress lines. However, to most other animals they are harmful. Horses and cows stabled over Geopathic Stress spirals may become sick or injury prone.

Some plants love GS. These include ivy, mushrooms, mistletoe, bindweed, foxgloves, nettles, docks and medicinal herbs. However, many fruit trees and plants will suffer. Twisted or stunted growth and gaps in hedges may be clues. Bare patches in lawns, moss and fungi, stunted or mutated growth in veggie gardens can be due to siting over lines of geopathic stress.

What's all this got to do with dowsing and psychic power?

While scientific instruments are not yet sensitive enough to register many of the harmful energies around us,

ANTHONY TALMAGE

Geopathic Stress can be detected by dowsing. And it can be cured by dowsing! A reminder: Dowsing is an ability that allows us to search for that which is hidden from view. Thousands of years ago human survival depended on the ability to find water and minerals so dowsing was a highly developed skill. This skill can be utilised to detect these dangerous subtle energies. The dowser uses his or her body as a detector and the presence of the energies is indicated by the movement of the dowsing tool.

As we've learned, these days these energies also include man-made electromagnetic high and low frequencies from telecommunication towers, electricity pylons, transformers, radar and radio towers and the myriad other transmissions which have become a part of modern life. Whether natural or artificial these energies can be bad, good or neutral. But the exciting thing for a dowser is that, besides being detected they can also be neutralized by dowsing. While there are gadgets and gizmos which will alert you to the presence and strength of the conventional energy spectrum – from gamma rays at one end to radio waves at the other – there is no instrument which will tell you if you are living or working over a natural 'noxious ray.' But the dowser has one – their physical body allied to their consciousness and then indicated by their dowsing tool.

Some consider that these subtle energies have a quality similar in nature to the meridians of 'chi' running through the human body. 'Chi' paths in the earth have been called 'dragonlines', 'song lines', 'spirit paths', 'energy leys' or 'ley lines'. Depending on the strength and character of the earth energies present, a location may be a healthy and beneficial one for human presence, it may be indifferent to human presence, or it may be potentially harmful and undermining to human health at all physical, emotional, mental or spiritual levels.

When the home or workplace of the affected person is neutralized, the Geopathic Stress conditions resolve themselves and the body begins to heal.

So, how do we dowsers do this? Different dowsing professionals use different methods. After locating a line of 'black energy' one dowser might divert the line by hammering metal stakes into the ground in a form of earth acupuncture. Another might place a crystal inside the house, using its energies to neutralize the detrimental influence. A more technically-savvy dowser could plug a device into a wall socket to balance the negative frequencies. Sometimes these methods work but often the beneficial effects wear off after a time and the householder is back to square one.

The method I use is one all dowsers, beginners or experienced, can use - mind power. I use my INTENT to convert the detrimental energies into beneficial ones. Confident that my consciousness has the power to affect energies I mentally 'order' the energies to change, or move, or dissolve – whichever seems appropriate. And you can do this, too. Remember, all human beings have tremendous power. Once you realize this and have confidence this faith can 'move mountains.' The dowser's ability is summed up in the Holy Bible, Matthew chapter 17, verse 20: "Jesus told them. 'I tell you the truth, if you had faith even as small as a mustard seed, you could say to this mountain, "Move from here to there," and it would move. Nothing would be impossible.'

The actual process for us dowsers is simple. Once you have found the source of the GS (excluding spirit infestation which I will come on to) hold your rods or pendulum in the search position and check that the detrimental energies are still where you previously located them. Your rods will cross or open, or your pendulum will swing. Then get into the Alpha state and focus your mind, picturing the energies pulsing away in front of you. Then, either out loud or silently, call on your Spirit Guide or Angel Helper and say something along the lines of: 'May all the benevolent Powers of Nature converge in this place to convert all detrimental energies in this entire house and garden, into beneficial energies for the benefit of X's family, their friends, pets, trees and plants, those who visit them and for all of benevolent life for now and into the future, for as long as is appropriate. In deep gratitude. Thank you.' You can vary the form of words to whatever you are comfortable with – they are spoken to re-inforce the power of your intent, which is doing all the hard work. In scientific terms you are 'collapsing the wave function' creating a different scene with changed vibrations. You can use this same methodology to move energy from one place to another. Believe. The wonderful thing about dowsing is that, once you have carried out your ritual you can use the rods or pendulum again to check whether you have been successful. I usually ask my rods 'Show me detrimental energy' as I walk into the previously stressed area. If I get no reaction I have succeeded. But, just to double check, I repeat the exercise saying, 'Show me beneficial energies.' The rods should cross enthusiastically.

But is the effect permanent? Or does it wear off like some of the physical clearing methods? On the whole it is permanent with one important proviso – what new detrimental energies are being created by the human inhabitants of the home? Just as the dowser has power to disperse energies, any human being can create detrimental energies with their negative thinking, self-limiting doubts or bad behaviour.

I was once asked to assess the energies in a cottage shared by a brother and sister who did not really get on very well. They had inherited the place from their parents who had lived in the property most of their lives before their deaths. I have rarely come across such a mélange of negative energies – the walls were severely cracked and stained with damp patches, the rooms were cluttered and my dowsing rods indicated swirling, detrimental vibrations everywhere. Some, I ascertained, were from underground streams about 10 metres beneath the house but most were lingering thought-forms and spirit attachments which had developed from the years of pessimism and misery from the old couple, added to by the more recent emotional tension between the siblings.

ANTHONY TALMAGE

I cleared all the negativity away and you could feel a new lightness in the air. It was almost as if the house itself was saying 'thank you' for clearing its dark, dank atmosphere. The brother and sister both commented how different the place felt. I wanted to tell them both that it would be best for everyone's sake if they stopped their personal war of attrition and changed their negative attitudes. But I didn't want to offend, so I related the story of a similar property, hoping they might see the similarity and change their ways. But, I fear they probably didn't. In that case, despite my spiritual spring clean, things will probably have gone back to as they were. I give householders a clean slate but it's up to them to keep it clean. The British Society of Dowsers has a register of members who specialise in diagnosing and curing homes and offices affected by these detrimental energies.

While many dowsers accept these energies as a given, some find it difficult to take on board that there are malevolent unseen forces vibrating all around us due to, perhaps, an underground stream 100 metres below ground. These practical dowsers are happy to detect the water, but are uncomfortable at the idea of 'noxious rays.' Imagine, then, how these stalwarts of the divining fraternity might regard another area of dowsing, which is meat and drink to us   psychics   –   spirit   attachments.

11 MEDITATION – DON'T JUST DO SOMETHING, SIT THERE!

An indispensable way of getting in touch with your inner psychic is through meditation – easier said than done when this frenetic world is demanding our undivided attention at all times. But, studies have shown that the simple act of meditating for a few minutes can help relieve anxiety, stress, insomnia, fatigue, and reduce blood pressure. Those are just some of the physical benefits. Meditation also offers mental and spiritual rewards so setting aside time for quietening the clamour is a must. It seems paradoxical but the more you are able to shut out the world and commune with the Absolute the better equipped you will be to improve your health, self-esteem, relationships, job and finances. This is because meditating gives you access to your unconscious and Higher Self which, in turn, is connected to All That Is, which means all knowledge, all information and all possibilities. Fifteen minutes of quiet meditation can be more valuable than hours of left brain fretting, worry and thinking. It's the Alpha State we want, although Theta will do very nicely, thank you. But, let's aim first at achieving a pleasant day-dreamy mood. This meditation exercise is an excellent introduction to meditation techniques.

1. Sit or lie comfortably. You may even want to invest in a meditation chair.

2. Close your eyes.

3. Make no effort to control the breath; simply breathe naturally.

4. Focus your attention on the breath and on how the body moves with each inhalation and exhalation. Notice the movement of your body as you breathe. Observe your chest, shoulders, rib cage and stomach. Make no effort to control your breath; simply focus your attention. If your mind wanders, return your focus back to your breath. Maintain this meditation practice for 2–3 minutes to start, and then try it for longer periods.

The 'Alpha Mode' exercise we looked at earlier is also a form of meditation and can alternate with the above.

If you want your meditation to achieve a concrete objective – like an improvement in your lifestyle, or to stop smoking, or lose weight, here's a more beefy exercise:

Choose your objective (say, losing weight)

This hinges on using the words '...I don't know how I come to be so confident in my ability to create and realise my hopes, wishes, dreams and desires...I only know that it is so now and I am fulfilled...'

Now organise the brain and the body to be in harmony to accept this idea.

Close your eyes...deep breath...relax...send your energy down into the earth...down, down, down...and ground. imagine roots are coming out the bottom of your feet connecting with the intelligence of the earth. the earth holds the wisdom of billions of years of knowledge and information, has the dna of all the bones of our ancestors, those who are thriving and succeeding, holds the key to mysteries of the world that we don't understand. tune in and tap into those mysteries and that knowledge. bring that knowledge up in the form of a shaft of light...up through your feet, up into your body and your solar plexus and up into your heart...take a deep breath and breath out sending that light out from your heart...align your purpose with love and harmony and joy...now we are going to move your consciousness up. let your eyes look up underneath your closed eyelids...this is replicating the rem...rapid eye movement, theta state...and then imagine moving out of your body up to the ceiling, up to the sky, gently, don't strain, and move that consciousness up and out through space, without your body. you move to a beam of light that's coming out of the centre of the universe and is just in front of you...you step into it and you find yourself moving out through our sky, into space, through the solar system, out past the milky way right to the edge of the galaxy where there's this void of blackness. you push through this black void and you find yourself in a brilliant, white luminosity, that contains all that there is, all the potential that is yours personally...and mentally just hear the words '...i don't know how i ...(put in your command) am going to achieve my perfect weight but i only know that it is so and i am fulfilled. i don't know how i come to be so confident in my ability to create and realise my hopes, wishes, dreams and desires, i only know that it is so now and i am fulfilled...' now expand out into an idea that is even greater, that serves a greater good for you and the world than you can even imagine...just allow yourself to remain in this thought. this is where you are receiving all this new information and knowledge, this is where you are organising the entire universe to come into harmony with you. now bring all this back down into your body, let your eyes relax and we're literally speaking to the cells of your body, your dna and your brain and we're saying, 'unwind, unwind, unwind my limits and my fears, my regrets, my judgements against myself...let them go and now in this beautiful, new space in you rewind, rewind, rewind   into   this   new   picture.

12 CHART DOWSING

Sometimes your answers while dowsing with pendulum or rod (are you still practising every day?) need to be more detailed than getting a 'yes' or 'no' or 'true' or 'false'. Once you get into the area of specifics – someone's health say, or which plants might do best in your garden, or what category of Geopathic Stress might exist in a certain location – you will need a chart.

This takes the form of a diagram, divided into sections representing percentages, probabilities, a health gauge, the alphabet and so on. You can buy books of these charts, which represent pretty well any topic you might want to address. Here's some of those in Dale Olson's book of charts to give you the idea:

Vitamins / Essential & Trace Minerals /Amino Acids

Food Supplements

Enzymes for Digestion

Nutrition & Food Allergies / Adverse Effects

Herbal Remedies

Flower Essence Remedies

Systems of the Body / Glandular (Endocrine) System

Source of Condition / Origin of Dis-ease / Dysfunction

Healing Remedies

Relationship Compatibility

Personal Motivators

Who is involved - their relationship to you

How to Change my Life

Chakras

Gemstones

Directions / Degrees / Distance.

House Inventory

Soil Chart

Business Decision analysis

The idea is you use your pendulum to point the way to the answer you are seeking. You swing it at a diagonal in the usual search position and allow it to settle at that angle. Then ask your question. For instance: 'What is the percentage likelihood that it will rain today?' The pendulum will slowly move to a new back-and-forth position, eventually settling over the correct figure. Of course you don't need to spend money buying charts – you can make your own and develop new ones as you gain experience or specialize in a particular area. There are some handy, free, starter charts which you can download from Juanita Ott's website mirrorwaters.com.

Or you can download and print off a typical 'general' chart from the acclaimed publication 'Letter to Robin – a Mini Course in Pendulum Dowsing' by Walt Woods, which has set hundreds of novice dowsers on the dowsing road. The link is lettertorobin.org.

Those of us interested in psychic matters will find charts an indispensable tool in our armoury.

13 DIVINING YOUR GUIDING SPIRIT

In using a dowsing chart, or in any other application of divining, the first thing you might want to do is contact your spirit guide who will be communicating through your pendulum. Of course, if you have not met your spirit guide here and now will be when you start working together for the first time! Before you start swinging your pendulum you need to establish a 'relationship' with that entity which is in another dimension. This means you need to know who he, or she, is. Oh dear! We seem to be going backwards. Just as we were on the brink of dowsing our chart we get side-tracked into a different aspect of the psychic realm.

But, make no mistake, building a relationship with your Spirit Guide is crucial, not just for getting the right answers from your dowsing tool, but also for protecting you from malevolent influences from other planes. So let's put dowsing our chart on hold and back up a bit to deal with the all-important topic of Spirit Guides. We all have them but we need to get to know what ours looks, sounds and behaves like.

At the risk of stating the obvious, you are not going to meet your spirit guide while racking up a score at the bowling alley, or in a noisy pub, or at a football match (even if your team's winning 8-nil). No, meeting your Guardian Angel or your Guiding Spirit will only happen when you have taken the time and trouble to get into the right spiritual mood. So let's give it a go. The meditation exercises mentioned earlier would be a good start. Once your brain is in the Alpha state, imagine walking along a country path across a field full of the flickering colours of different species of butterfly. As you walk, be aware of the smell of grass in your nostrils and a gentle, warm summer breeze on your skin. After you cross the field you enter a friendly wood. The trees all round you seem to offer a safe haven and the brightness of the open countryside gives way to a softer, shadier hue.

As you continue walking it gets noticeably darker but you can still see the reassuring blue of the sky and dappled sunlight though the canopy of the trees. You notice more wildlife around you – rabbits contentedly eating the lower leaves of saplings, squirrels scurrying upwards, a fox lopes across your line of sight. Everything speaks of harmony; nature in complete balance. In the distance you see a shaft of sunlight shining down through a clearing in which sits a small, crooked cottage. You notice the path you are on leads directly to its front door, as though you have been led here. The door is ajar and you gently push it open and step inside. You walk down a passage to another door at the end. Gently you ease this door open and see a traditional cottage kitchen – a range against one wall, a sink and draining board against another, and a window looking out onto the wood beyond. But the room is dominated by a large, old pine table behind which sits a figure.

The sun shining through the window means the figure is in silhouette; you can't make out whether it's a man or woman. You notice to your surprise that you are not in the least afraid or even apprehensive. There is a chair opposite the figure and something tells you to sit down. As you walk towards the chair you suddenly know this figure is your Guiding Spirit. As you sit you can see the face; a voice speaks your name…

At this point you are free to ask this figure any question you like – its name, how long it has known you (this could go back several lifetimes), whether it's male or female, whether it is prepared to help you with your dowsing, whether it prefers to communicate at other times clairvoyantly or by a clairaudient, telepathic dialogue and so on. When the conversation ends, don't forget to thank him or her and retrace your steps…down the corridor, out through the front door, down the path, through the trees, across the field, right back to where you started. Then, mentally count backwards from five to zero and open your eyes. When you are fully back into this world, and this is very important, write down everything you can remember about the conversation in the cottage because, like some dreams, the detail could evaporate as you get back into the routine of daily living.

Now, each time you dowse, mentally begin by greeting your Guide and asking for his/her help with your dowsing project. In the final analysis it is up to them to tell you what they want you to know.

14 YOUR GUARDIAN (AND OTHER) ANGELS

Your Spirit Guide is not necessarily the same thing as your Guardian Angel. In fact it is more than likely that they are completely different beings. We talked earlier about these immortal messengers who mediate between God and humanity. On a close and personal level we all have a Guardian Angel and there are bands of angels in the jobless queue who are only too willing to help out if we ask. So how do we do this?

There are literally thousands of rituals which you can find on the internet, which proves that there is no single, guaranteed way, to make contact with your own, special angelic helper. But, like contacting your Spirit Guide, you need to set aside some time, and find a suitable place, to be quiet. Being a dowser gives you a head start in linking up with the angelic realm because the act of dowsing itself gets the brain into the right Alpha state. And then there's

INTENT. This keeps cropping up in our dowsing activities and the reason is that INTENT is the equivalent of broadcasting a message to the universe saying that you need a helping hand, or even that you are ready, willing and able to make a contribution to the Cosmic Plan.

So step 1 is ask your pendulum if it is possible at this moment to make contact with your Guardian Angel. If the answer is 'No' it will be for a good reason, so try again later. If the answer is 'Yes' go to Step 2, which is to continue to dowse in a spirit of faith and trust. While whirling your pendulum in a 'Yes' motion ask, 'Please give me a message.' Allow your mind to completely relax and just wait for a voice to answer which might come clairaudiently, or you may get a picture in your mind, or a feeling of knowing. You may tell yourself you are making it up but continue in an attitude of acceptance. You will hear words of love, comfort, and guidance. Step 3 is to give thanks respectfully and say you wish to build a relationship with your angel, who will be there whenever you need it. As you continue to practice, your communication will become easier and deeper.

Jean Slatter, in her book 'Hiring the Heavens' says that we all should fully engage with the heavenly realm to solve our practical, earthly issues. She says: 'When we see ourselves as divinely sanctioned creatures, something quite amazing happens. The transformation is unmistakable. We live life from a different vantage point. We recognize our authority to summon the vast resources of the Heavens and all of the eager spiritual assistance that's available for everything we do. We discover that all conceivable problems can be solved by our connection to this incredible power. With this new awareness we can shape our lives purposefully, creating joy and fulfillment with such ease that it feels like a miracle. From now on our lives can be deliberate, joyful expressions of the infinite Source of all creation and possibilities. Heaven can finally be brought down to Earth.'

Jean approaches enlisting help from the Heavens as a kind of hiring process, as you might engage a cleaner, or an interior decorator, a chef, a babysitter or an accountant. She claims that for every earthly 'job' there is a spiritual counterpart waiting in the wings. Try it.

15 TIME-TRAVEL DOWSING

Yes, you can go backwards and forwards in time with your pendulum or rods. Some call this retro-cognition (peering back into the past) and precognition (knowing impending events before they happen).

You can dowse the age of an ancient monument, sacred site or stone circle. Strictly speaking this is not going back in time – it's just staying in the present and using the pendulum or rods to guage how long something's been in existence. I'll come to real time travel in a minute. But dealing with aging something first – that's what archaeological, or earth energy dowsers do when they are exploring the man-made remains of a structure. If it's a stone circle, say, the dowser will ask the pendulum...Was this site constructed more than a thousand years ago? If the answer's 'Yes' he will go on to ask...More than 1500 years..? More than 2,000...? And, by a process of elimination, he will narrow the age down to the exact number of years in the past our ancient ancestors were sweating and heaving the stones into place. Then he might ask, 'Was it built as a location for worship? An astronomical observatory? Were there human sacrifices here...?' And so on. By the time you've finished, you will be able to build up a detailed picture of the location. Yes, it was built for spiritual reasons 3,000 years ago. It took five years to lay down and served as an energy amplifier for the tribe's shaman. Later, prominent people were buried there. Two thousand years ago the site was pillaged and some stones were removed. Since then it has been undisturbed and has been a magnet for pilgrims from all over Europe. The picture you paint will be as detailed as the questions you ask.

The same principles apply to more recent human habitation – a Bronze Age or Roman settlement, for instance. The real time traveling that a dowser can do is known by the name of remanence dowsing, which is tracing the etheric outline of an object long gone, or following the invisible trail of someone's steps sometimes years after they had been there. Like map dowsing (more later) it's a concept that's hard to get your head round. How can anyone today detect the shape or position of something that was there hundreds of years ago but of which there is no physical trace today?

A typical example, for instance, is the retired accountant who uses a metal coat-hanger as his dowsing rod to locate the exact position of the walls, windows and doorways of churches and abbeys that fell down long ago whose only remains are now either covered by grass and earth or just plain gone. While archaeologists might find enough to verify there had been some kind of place of worship there, the accountant-dowser can trace the outline of a complex building complete with nave, altar, chancel and arcade. This phenomenon, of finding a memory of something that has vanished and left no trace of itself, is the 'remanence' (the tendency for conditions to remain). And this remanence applies to everything physical that has ever been on our planet. So a confident and experienced dowser can detect the energies and track the route taken by a dinosaur on its way to drink, or discern the exact spot Harold died at the Battle of Hastings. This is because everything in existence has a unique frequency, like we each have unique fingerprints or DNA. The dowser can ask to be shown the frequency of the above dinosaur and there it will be.

Experience as a dowser is essential, though, if you are going to specialize in this area, as remanence creates a trap for the unwary. To give an example: if someone in your family has lost their car keys and asks you, as the nearest handy dowser, to find them, your rods may take you straight to the hall table where they usually are but the keys are no-where to be found. That's because you are detecting the 'remanence' of the keys and not the real thing. So, it's important in a case like this to be specific with your question '...Where are my daughter's missing car keys NOW.' Until you specify exactly what you want, as far as your rods (really your intuition) are concerned the energies in the astral world are as real as the energies of the here and now.

When it comes to divining the future there seems to be a governing factor in the process which you might call Need or Greed? If you try to dowse the numbers of the Lottery, you will fail. This is because whoever the God of Dowsing is He/She has decreed that no-one must use dowsing to further their own ends unfairly. Dowsing has to be ethical. So, getting rich quick is a non-starter. Putting all your savings on the 3.10 at Chepstow will only ensure you end up with no savings. However, to dowse what the weather will be on the day of your daughter's wedding in six months is quite acceptable – it's a need that will harm no-one. So, work out for yourself what your limitations are and go for it. Will I get an interview for the dream job I have applied for? Is OK. What questions will I be asked? You're pushing your luck. If it's fair, if it's ethical, you'll get an accurate answer. If it's unfair and unethical, you might be taught a lesson. You have not become a dowser to gain an advantage for yourself at the expense of someone else. Hopefully, you will use your dowsing skills to serve.

16 MAP DOWSING

Map dowsing is the first cousin of pre- and retro-cognition. This is using a pendulum to locate places, people or substances anywhere in the world without leaving your house. You encountered this in the foreword of this book, which recounted the amazing experience of Dr Elizabeth Mayer and her daughter's stolen harp. No-one knows how map dowsing works but it does. 'Ordinary' dowsing can be explained as the mind tuning into certain magnetic fields, or frequencies given off by physical objects. But map dowsing is more akin to a psychic reading where the map acts as a device to focus the mind and the pendulum becomes a psychic amplifier. The map becomes a symbol of the city, town, country or terrain in which you need to find something. Learning this skill can achieve amazing results.

At one end a map can be a large-scale Ordinance Survey grid or at the other simply a sketch that represents an area, location or even a room plan. Among other things the skill can be used for:

Prospecting for minerals and gemstones;

Space clearing and identifying noxious environmental energies;

Finding lost objects, pets or people;

Siting a water well;

Treasure hunting (but not for personal gain at the expense of others);

Evaluating a person or animal using the drawing as a surrogate;

Map dowsing is mostly about locating things. Once you find them on the map or sketch, you can locate them in the real world. The technique is the same regardless of what you are seeking.

There are several common methods used for map dowsing. Here are a couple of basic ones:

After focusing your mind on the 'target,' clearly visualizing it, slowly slide a ruler or something with a straight edge from left to right across the map or sketch, asking your dowsing tool to indicate when the leading edge of the ruler hits whatever it is you are seeking. Then draw with a pencil a line from top to bottom of the map.

Then do the same exercise but this time moving the

straight edge from top to bottom of the search area again asking your dowsing devise to tell you when you have reached the target. Where the two lines cross is your location. A variation of this method is to run the ruler from opposite corners.

Another technique is to ask your pendulum to swing towards the target and follow this direction until the swing changes to a circular movement. One dowser I know has made himself a miniature L rod which points at the location as he moves it round the periphery of the map. When it locks on to a definite direction he slowly follows the line until   the   rod   swings   to   one   side.

17 TALKING WITH ANIMALS

No, you're not about to become the children's fictional character Doctor Doolittle, who could speak to animals in their own languages. But, yes, with your dowsing tool you can connect, mind to mind, with your pet companion.

And this is how you do it: Put one hand on your pet to make the connection between your energies, And, use the other hand to control your dowsing device – probably the pendulum is most appropriate but you could use an L-rod. Remember, for results that are terrific it pays to be specific. So be very careful how you word your questions. Your biggest challenge will be to adopt a really neutral mind-set because you are likely to feel emotional about your animal. Adopt a detached interest; separate your emotions from the job in hand; try to think as you dowse, 'I don't know and I don't care – I am open to whatever the answer is.'

Say the animal is your pet dog, Daisy, and she

seems to have a painful and stiff leg. Is it arthritis? Or a sprain? Is it a joint problem? Or could it be a torn ligament? To get to the root of the issue you need to phrase your questions to drill down to the central cause. Swinging your pendulum in the search position you might begin by asking: Is Daisy's limp caused by a physical problem? It might seem obvious that it is, but there could be an emotional or mental cause behind it. If the answer is 'Yes' start the process of elimination. Is the cause of Daisy's limp skeletal damage? 'No.' Is it muscular? 'No.' Is it connected with a ligament? 'No.' Is the problem with her foot? 'Yes.' Has it suffered a recent trauma? 'Yes.' Did it happen while she was out walking? 'Yes.' Are all the pads affected? 'Yes.' Are the toes injured? 'No.' Is the damage permanent? 'No.' So it would seem Daisy hurt her foot in some way as she scampered about in the undergrowth. You can then address Daisy directly: Daisy, did you put your foot awkwardly down a rabbit hole? 'No.' Did you catch it in some branches in the bushes? 'Yes.' As a responsible dog owner you will now examine Daisy's foot carefully and note if she flinches when you hold it. You might then decide to confine her to gentle exercise and see if nature heals her. Or, if she is in obvious pain, you will take her to the vet for treatment.

If you begin to use dowsing regularly with your animal friend, you will certainly improve your understanding of him or her. And you will have a more harmonious relationship. You may save money too if your dowsing tells you it's not serious and will correct itself, if treated lovingly at home.

18 TALKING WITH PLANTS

As with animals, you can talk with plants, too. Just because they do not scamper about and appear to respond only to environmental conditions, does not mean they do not have a kind of intelligence that you can tap into. In fact Grover Cleveland "Cleve" Backster, Jr. caused a sensation in America when he proved that plants could read his mind! Backster, who died in 2013 at the age of 89, was America's foremost expert in the polygraph, the lie-detector which works by measuring the electrical resistance in a human being's skin. During a boring day at the office in 1966 he connected the electrodes of the machine up to one of his philodendron plants to measure the time it took for water to reach the large leaves. He noticed that the plant was measuring what, in a human subject, would be classified as excitement. He then tried different things with the leaf that had the polygraph electrode attached - even sticking it into a cup of hot coffee. The plant showed no other reactions and even seemed to be getting bored. Backster, too, was getting bored with the experiment but decided to do one last, dramatic, act. He would burn the leaf. He didn't have any matches so he left the room to find some. When he came back, he noticed the plant's readings jumping all over. Backster was astounded when he concluded that just the thought of burning the leaf was enough to throw the plant into a state of fear. A variation on the experiment proved the plant would sense the intended assault whether it was in the next room or even miles away. The process was performed numerous times by different people and the same results were happening although, after time, the philodendron began to realize it was just a test and wouldn't really be burned!

There followed 36 years of research which culminated in Backster writing a book about his experiences which became a world best-seller. He had termed a plant's sensitivity to thoughts 'primary perception,' and entitled his book, Primary Perception: Biocommunication With Plants. Perhaps an even more important revelation that emerged from Backster's later experiments, which he details in the book, was that it was not only plants that respond to our emotions and intents. So do severed leaves, eggs (fertilized or not), yogurt, and human cell samples. He found, for instance, that white cells taken from a person's mouth and placed in a test tube still responded electrochemically to the donor's emotional states, even when the donor was out of the room, out of the building, or out of the country! He stumbled on this new dimension to bio-communication when he poured boiling water down the sink. His plant seemed to react again. What could hot water going down a sink have to do with a response from his measurements of the philodendron? It had to be that live microscopic organisms in the drain were being killed by the hot water – and the plant was reacting in sympathy. He was astonished that bacteria could emit signals that could be received many feet away by another life form.

These discoveries opened up a new paradigm in science, ecology and healing.

You don't need a polygraph to communicate with your house plants, veg patch or rose garden – the humble pendulum will do. Gently touching the pot plant you can ask: 'Is this the best place in the room for you to thrive?' If the answer is 'No' either ask your pendulum to indicate the direction of the best location (it will swing back and forth pointing the way) or you can hold one L-rod in the search position and turn slowly in a circle until it 'sticks' in one direction. Then follow it until it swings sideways, as if it was crossing with its invisible partner. That is the position in the house where your pot plant will do best. You can repeat this exercise in the garden for your outdoor plants.

If a plant is looking sickly you can ask it was is wrong: 'Do you need water', 'Am I over-watering you?' 'Is there too much shade'? 'Is there too much sunlight?' 'Are you being suffocated by other plants nearby?' If your mind is in a state of 'relaxed concentration' as you dowse, you will get the right answers and your garden and house plants will flourish.

19 TALKING WITH STONES

Yes, you can even talk to stones. And the idea is not as mad as people might think. Remember, according to the Big Bang Theory, we all came from the same original source. So we are all interconnected. Later, as nothingness began to coalesce into atoms, those atoms became different things – dinosaurs, insects, fish, birds, animals, people. And, as the famed Double Slit Experiment now demonstrates, the smaller, constituent parts of atoms – particles – have a consciousness. Every atom is conscious. Just because some of them may be inert as part of a rock, does not mean there is not some form of intelligence there. The posh word for it is 'panpsychism.' And it's this intelligence that we tap into with when we dowse.

To help you communicate in the most effective way, here are my top tips for dowsing at a sacred/megalithic site:

1 Quieten your rational mind - if you try to make sense of dialoguing with the stones, you wont;

2 Tune in to the consciousness of the stones and allow it to interact with yours;

3 Be aware (but don't analyse) how you feel on an emotional level;

Then, as you move about the site, ask whatever questions you feel appropriate - eg

When was the site built?

What was its purpose - Religious? Ceremonial? Astronomical? Other?

Do the stones retain their power?

Does water run beneath the site? Does this feed the site's energies?

What energy lines run through and around the site?

Do the stones communicate with other sacred sites?

Can the stones help me? Can I help them?

Is there a special spot for me to stand today?

Is there a special stone ready to feed its energy to me today?

What message is the stones communicating to me today?

Do the stones have a healing purpose?

Can they help me with my healing purpose?

Is there anything else of interest for me to find? If so show me where.

N.B. Always ask permission of the Spirit of Place or the Guardian of the Site before you enter or do any work.

And remember to protect yourself before entering the site and starting your dialogue.

20 BEWARE! THAT POT HAS POWER

Earlier we talked about Geopathic Stress and I mentioned one contributor can be something called a 'Power Object.' This can be any item – a ring, say, or an ornament, a vase, book, painting, stone, an item of clothing or anything that can be touched. It is something that contains energies 'transmitted' to it by a life form – usually a human being. Gifted psychics known as psychometrists can 'read' the information held by the object, sometimes hundreds of years after the information was impressed on it. Sometimes the energy held by this power object is malevolent and can infect a home or office with bad vibrations, causing bad luck, illness, disharmony and unhappiness. I once had a telephone call from a woman who'd been beset by pains in her stomach for no apparent reason. Her doctor had sent her for tests and all proved negative. In desperation she called me to see if I could dowse what the problem was. I asked her, 'Have you recently brought an item into your home that wasn't there before?' 'No,' she replied, 'nothing at all.' My pendulum told me there had been something so I asked her if she was sure. And to think back over the last few weeks to see if there was anything that was there now that hadn't been there when she was well. She thought for a while and then said, ' Oh, there is this antique ring I bought at an auction a few weeks ago. I'm wearing it now.' I asked her how long ago her pains had started. It turned out they had begun shortly after the auction. So I dowsed again. Eventually, I told her that the ring had belonged to an elderly woman that had died of stomach cancer. 'Take the ring off, put it into a drawer, and see what happens,' I suggested. A few days later she rang to say the pains had cleared up completely. The previous owner of the ring had unwittingly transmitted the signature of her suffering onto the ring and it was being 'picked up' by a later wearer. I then remotely cleared the resonances, neutralising the ring's energies. The woman moved to Scotland and, as far as I know, had no further health issues with her stomach.

A power object can be anything that human thoughts and feelings have been embedded in. In his book 'Heal Your Home', dowsing professional Adrian Incledon-Webber sites the different power objects that he's come across that are centres of negativity. He says, 'Can you imagine, for instance, sitting in a sweat shop in the Far East making yet another teddy bear for the European market - then, at the end of the week, getting only a few rupees? I cannot think for a minute that you would be happy, frustrated yes, resentful yes, dislike for the teddy bear Oh yes! Does this make for a happy toy? I don't think so.'

The author then goes on to other items which could be found in pretty well any home, 'Inherited heirlooms can, and often will be, power artefacts, bringing detrimental energies from past generations to affect us in the present. A chair that has seen generations of misery can only hold bad feelings. A mirror that has been owned by a person not happy with their looks can easily reflect detrimental thought patterns. Even modern items of furniture can be cause for concern. If a person lifting, say, a chest of drawers slips and drops it on his foot, the anger has to go somewhere, and it is more than likely the chest will be the target of his ire.

'Old dining tables can often be a source of stored up detrimental energy, with several generations of children having sat around the table in a formal way - having to endure endless comments from their judgemental elders. 'Sit up straight', 'Don't eat with your mouth open', 'Hold your knife and fork properly', 'Why aren't you working harder at school?' And so on. You cannot blame any child from fleeing the table at high speed to avoid the interrogation! The longer the detrimental comments are made, the more the table and chairs will soak up the negativity. 'Gradually, these objects will become so powerfully charged that they can, and will, start to influence those gathered around the table. No sooner than you sit down you will begin to feel irritable, picking up on past energies, and start making snide comments - until the whole table is in uproar for no apparent reason.'

Adrian goes on to explain that wooden carvings,

ornaments and gifts brought back from our holidays abroad can also be affected. 'There was a classic case of a lady client who bought an old totem carving from a street seller in Africa. The whole of her family thought that it was ugly, but she loved it, and she hung it in her study when she returned from the trip. Within a few days she started feeling faint, and she developed a bad headache that just would not go away. 'I feel as though something is inside my head and I am experiencing strange thoughts, I am not myself', she told me on the telephone. 'I also feel as though something is watching me all the time; it's beginning to freak me out!' Now, this conversation took place about six weeks after her return from Africa. She had seen a Doctor, who prescribed tranquilisers, as he felt that her symptoms were stress-related (she did have a demanding job in the City), and he was considering a brain scan, as the headache would just not go away.'

If you want comprehensive coverage of all the psychic dangers that lurk in our living environment I recommend Adrian's book.

But power objects are not just about bad vibrations. The opposite is just as true. There are many items in the home that emanate good vibrations – paintings, sculpture, a favourite armchair of a kind, gentle soul, crystals, even the water that comes out of the taps; if it has come from a source with positive resonances, they will be brought into your home. The important thing for you as a psychic to keep in mind is to think positive thoughts and feel positive. When a negative thought pops into your head make a point of turning it into something positive. Instead of, 'Oh no, not more rain' as you open the curtains in the morning, try, 'More rain, which means the reservoirs are filling and there'll be no shortages this year.'

So, at the deepest level, as quantum science now proves, reality is a sea of living energy, vibrating at various frequencies. When you break matter down to the smallest level, there is nothing solid at all! A table, a river, an apple, your body itself is made up of vibrating wavelengths of energy that appear as solid form.

And the things you don't see that aren't solid, such as music, colour, sunlight, your thoughts and feelings, etc., are also all energy, vibrating at different frequency levels.

When you experience the world as energy, including you and the people and situations in your life, a whole new dimension opens up that's akin to stepping into wonderland! You realize just how magical life is, and how malleable too!

21 YOUR BODY CANNOT LIE

And talking of magic, this would be a good time to explain a magical technique that anyone can learn in minutes but which will give you accurate answers to life's daily challenges. And I don't mean your pendulum. Is that politician lying to me? (No, this is probably not a good question as the answer is almost certainly, Yes!). Let's try, 'Is this food bad for me?' Or, 'Has my friend Jane got Irritible Bowel Syndrome? Or, 'Should I apply for this job? The answers can be found through a technique called muscle testing. Muscle-testing is known professionally as Applied Kinesiology and, basically, deals with strong or weak muscle responses to questions. A weak response is 'No' and a strong 'Yes.' Strong is 'True', weak is 'False.' Simple. In fact some say it is a more accurate way of divining than dowsing. In his book Power vs Force, the Hidden Determinents of Human Behaviour, Dr David Hawkins details how anyone can instantly determine the truth or falsehood of any statement or supposed fact. Dr. Hawkins, who worked as a 'healing psychiatrist' during a long and distinguished career, uses theoretical concepts from particle physics, nonlinear dynamics, and chaos theory to support his study of human behaviour. His form of muscle-testing involves two people -- one who holds out his/her arm to the side, parallel to the ground, and one who asks a simple yes/no question about an object, person or idea. Depending on the answer the person holding their arm out will either test 'strong' or 'weak.' I know this sounds too good to be true but it works!

Dr Hawkins contends that the answers are correct because in this Quantum World all things are connected, and that all events, actions, thoughts and emotions are written into the Akashic record and that as participants in this universe, we all have access to that Database. Thus through muscle testing we have the ability to get the answer to any question we can formulate (except the future). Wow! So how can you, as a dowsing beginner and psychic student, have the secret of all knowledge?

Try this exercise and then build on it to create your own system: Find a willing partner and ask him/her (let's say 'her' as it avoids clumsy sentence construction) to stand and face towards the wall of a room without focusing on any particular part of it. Stand behind her and ask her to hold out her right arm horizontal to the floor. She should not make a tight fist, but let her hand remain relaxed.

Now you place the first two fingers of one hand lightly on her arm, just above the wrist.

Put your free hand on her opposite shoulder to support her.

Tell her, 'I'm going to have you make a statement, and then I'm going to press down on your arm. I want you to resist me by holding your arm right where it is; try to prevent me from pushing your arm down.'

Have your partner state her name. If it is Katy, for example, she would say, 'My name is Katy.'

Perform the muscle test by smoothly and steadily increasing the pressure downward on

Katy's arm, going from a light touch to fairly firm pressure within about 3 seconds.

The shoulder joint should stay 'locked' and should not give way.

Some tips

1 Don't use too much strength, only what you need to get your answer. Think finesse, not force.

2 Smoothly increase the force from zero to firm over about three seconds.

3 Keep your fingers in the correct position. If you place your fingers on the bones of Katy's wrist, her arm will weaken because the body will attempt to protect the wrist bones. You want your fingers to be just above the bony prominence on the back of the hand on the little finger side,

just above the wrist – roughly where a wristwatch strap would be.

4 Remember that your partner has to be willing to be tested. If their attitude is cynical or sceptical, it won't work. Don't waste your time with people who don't want to be helped, or who are not open to being helped. Let's assume that Katy is as interested in the experiment as you are.

You can try different arm positions to see what works best for you and whoever you are working on. Another option would be for Katy to hold her arm out to the front rather than straight out to the side.

If you are ever working with a person who tests strong no matter what you do, they might be dehydrated. Get them to drink a glass of water, then try again.

Once you have established what the response to a true statement feels like, try asking Katy to say her name is Freda. She should then test weak. Now you're getting into your stride. Use your L-rods to find the nearest detrimental energy spiral and get Katy to stand over it and muscle test again. She should be weak. Move her a few feet to one side and repeat – she should be strong again. Now get her to hold something like a bottle of bleach and hold it to her stomach. She will test weak. Swop it for an orange and (provided she's not allergic to oranges) she will test strong. Now move to questions that you don't know the answer to and see how you get on '…Is this room a healthy place for indoor plants?' 'Would that job I'm thinking of applying for be the right career move for me?' You will notice that we are now asking direct questions, not making statements. That's ok so long as Katy has accepted she is answering on your behalf. Or you could stick with statements – choose whatever seems right. After a little practice, muscle-testing can be an uncannily accurate way of getting the right answer – people will think you are psychic!

The magic of muscle-testing doesn't end here, though, because with surrogate and proxy testing you can even use someone else as a substitute for the person (or animal) you're trying to test. Both methods are very simple and take two people, plus the person (or animal) you are testing.

Anyone who is testable can act as surrogate for anyone else.

These two testing methods differ in that, while surrogate testing is used to test an untestable person who is physically present (say an infant), proxy testing allows you to test a person who is not present, and who can indeed be literally anywhere in the world.

Surrogate Testing

The first step in doing surrogate testing is to make sure that the surrogate herself, is testable. Do this by simply having the surrogate make a yes or no, true or false statement followed by a muscle test. Then go ahead as follows:

To make the connection, the surrogate simply touches or holds hands with the subject. Within a few seconds after their initial physical contact, the surrogate and the subject will be energetically connected and testing will be possible. Once this connection is made, you will ask questions of the subject or have the subject make the appropriate statements, but the muscle you're testing belongs to the surrogate, not the subject.

Have the subject say their name in the form of a statement, 'My name is (say, Janet)' Muscle test the surrogate, who should test strong.

Next, have the subject make an incongruent statement by saying, 'My name is (say, Joan)' using any name that is not their own.

Muscle test the surrogate. The surrogate should test weak at this point. If not, repeat the exercise until they do. Once the surrogate tests weak when the subject makes an incongruent statement, the connection has been made and further testing may go ahead.

Surrogate testing is the perfect solution for animals. Let's say you want to test your horse. Simply ask the surrogate to touch the horse. Then direct your questions to the horse and test the surrogate to get the responses.

Surrogate testing also works for someone who is unconscious, or even in a coma. Even if the person is unresponsive or unable to communicate, their subconscious mind is still at work; it never sleeps.

Proxy Testing

A proxy is someone who acts as a substitute. In proxy testing, the proxy temporarily 'becomes' the person being tested. By voluntarily putting themselves into the position of standing in for someone else, a proxy can be tested as if they were the subject of the testing, allowing their body to be used to benefit the subject.

Proxy testing is most useful when you want to help someone who is not present or who is inaccessible for some reason. Remember Quantum Entanglement? Distance doesn't matter!

As in any other type of muscle testing, you must make sure that the person who will be acting as proxy is testable.

To establish an energetic connection between Katy and (say) Brian Smith, Katy should affirm, 'My name is Brian Smith.' Now perform a muscle test. This statement will most likely elicit a weak muscle response at first. But, keep trying and gradually Katy's mind will accept that she is, temporarily, Brian Smith. Once the energetic connection is made the muscle test will suddenly become strong.

At this point, everything that Katy is being tested on it is actually Brian who is responding, however far away he may be. (This is a great example of you using your psychic abilities).

In both surrogate and proxy testing once you have

completed the questioning you must <u>never</u> forget to 'break the connection' – in this case between Katy and Brian otherwise Katy risks suffering from some of Brian's emotional weaknesses. So get Katy to state that she is Katy and once she tests strong the link is severed. Do this every time you surrogate or proxy test.

Muscle-testing could make a whole book in itself but at this stage it is enough that you have understood the importance of the technique and are prepaired to make it part of your own working practices.

22 WATER – ELIXIR OF LIFE

We talked earlier of the importance of being properly hydrated. This means drinking enough water on a regular basis. Water is another taken-for-granted miracle substance. You may not realize it but it can hold the key to your future health and good fortune. In the western world water is such an underrated and under-appreciated liquid. In Third World countries and Africa having it is, literally, a life saver. But, aside from it being essential to sustain life it is a miraculous – yes miraculous – substance. Every psychic should know the magic of water. Here are some ways in which water is magical, even mystical:

Every one of water's properties is unique and they do not easily fit into the general laws of physics.

According to science, water has 67 anomalous properties.

Water expands when cooled – the opposite of all other substances.

Water has highest surface tension of all liquids.

Water is the only substance on Earth that exists in 3 different states - solid, liquid and gas.

Water is the most powerful solvent on Earth.

Water can rise up hundreds of feet into the air in the trunks of giant trees against tens of atmospheres. How?

Because of water, a plant shoot at the moment of germination can develop 400 atmospheres of pressure and can easily break through asphalt.

Water molecules cluster like little magnets

These clusters have a 'memory.'

Water records the whole history of its relationship with the world as if on magnetic tape. Water of course remains water. But its structure, like a nervous system, reacts to any irritation.

Water reacts to subtle energy which explains the phenomenon of homeopathy where, while not a physical vestige of a substance remains in the solution, the electromagnetic signature of the substance remains active. Where the properties of water becomes of interest to the psychic is where it demonstrates it is sensitive to human emotions. Positive emotions projected toward water increases the water's energy. Negative emotions projected towards water reduces the water's energy and creates radical changes in its qualities. This is why underground streams become the 'black lines' of geopathic stress – the water has picked up negative emotions and continues to feed them along its path. These negative energies can be hundreds of years old. And if water can pick up and store emotion it is the water content in every human being that makes that person transmitters and receivers of good or bad vibrations.

Humans are about 70 per cent water. So what resonances in the environment that might affect water will affect a person. Water treatment processes in towns and cities might completely recycle all water supplied to homes and places of work. Though all the physical pollutants may be removed, the 'information fields' from the pollutants still remain and, like in the dilution process used in homeopathy, may have even stronger effects.

Modern science maintains that the water structure of each person's body is identical to the structure of the water in the place where they were born. Therefore, our internal connection to our place of birth is preserved throughout our life.

In the human brain, prayer and intention happen at a frequency which matches the Schumann pulse of the planet, which is 7.83 Hz. Since water is so sensitive to human emotions, make sure you use your intent to transmute any bad vibrations in your food or drink into positive ones. You can do this with a pendulum. Or you can simply focus your thoughts. The principle is the same as saying grace before meals. If you have positive thoughts and project them towards your food and drink you will be taking in positive energy. By contrast, if you project negative vibrations you are polluting your own bodies.

Water, no matter where it is, can react to the outside stimulus of any other portion of that same structured water no matter its location. These identical waters can be imprinted with very subtle energy. This is a quantum physics principle called 'action at a distance.' Since water has connection beyond boundaries of distance, it is believed that all human beings have 'remote communication' due to the water in our bodies.

Dr Masaru Emoto, in his book Messages from Water claims that the molecular structure of water can be changed just by sticking positive or negative words on the outside of the container - hate causes an ugly rearranging of molecules and love does the opposite. Can it be that in some magic way these words are understood by the water? I believe it is much more likely that the thoughts of the writer were imprinted on the words and it is this imprint that is picked up by the water - thus the resonant signature of cures for any ailment can be 'called up' by the human mind using the principle of quantum entanglement. Once a mind has locked onto the 'target' it sends an intention to cure and this intention is transmitted to the recipient.

Water is the source of life and the most valuable substance on the planet. Our body can work effectively only if it gets the necessary amount of water and minerals. That 70 per cent water that the body contains must be retained for optimal health. Thus, besides being essential for our health, keeping ourselves properly hydrated is an essential for dowsers. Dehydration is a severe medical condition that may cause a wide range of health problems. The importance of drinking enough water gained almost global recognition after the publication of a book called, Your Body's Many Cries for Water by Dr Fereydoon Batmanghelidj. Based on 20 years of clinical and scientific research into the role of water in the body, the book explains a breakthrough discovery that Unintentional Chronic Dehydration(UCD) produces stress, chronic pains and many painful degenerative diseases. Dry mouth is not the only sign of dehydration; If you are thirsty, it is already too late. Your body has already suffered some internal damage. Dr Batmanghelidj had been held for years as a political prisoner in Iran. As the only doctor, he was ordered by the guards to treat all the illnesses among his fellow inmates. But there were no drugs available. When a man was brought to him with a severe stomach ulcer, and in great pain, Dr Batmanghelidj tried to comfort the man by pretending that he had a cure. He told the man to drink a glass of water every few hours. To his astonishment, the man's pain receded and the ulcer eventually healed. When the doctor was arraigned before the judge prior to his execution, he asked if his notes could be passed on to the medical profession. The judge was so impressed by the doctor's researches that he commuted the death sentence to a further period in prison and Dr Batmanghelidj continued his work. When the time came for his release he begged the judge to allow him to stay to complete his research. This was granted and, when he was eventually freed, he took his discoveries to America where he wrote his book.

He claimed that drinking the correct amount of water each day would prevent and reverse conditions such as allergies, heartburn, back pain, arthritis, colitis pain, migrant headaches. It would also combat premature aging and help weight loss. The doctor recommended a person drink half the amount each day that the body weighed in ounces. In other words if you weigh 140 pounds you should drink 70 ounces of water each day – about eight average glasses.

Healing processes in our body are impossible without water. Our body has a unique healing ability but it needs at least 70 per cent water to function efficiently. Our brain is about 80% water and is a vital organ that controls every process in the body. The electrical signals are sent and received through our nervous systems to help the brain do its job. Distortion of the electrical signals is linked to such disorders as Chronic Fatigue, Alzheimer's Disease, Attention Deficit Disorder and Depression.

We all know that water is essential for life. However, probably because of its abundance and simple chemical composition, we often regard this tasteless and odourless substance as being important, but quite simple and ordinary. Scientifically, it is the exact opposite. It appears to show extremely complex and unusual behavior. It is the most studied substance on Earth. Yet, scientists are still puzzling over its strange properties. Even the best computers we have today cannot simulate all of the different properties of water.

The strangeness of water starts with the fact that it exists at all. Water, being composed of two fairly light atoms (hydrogen and oxygen), should be in the gas phase at the usual temperature ranges that exist in our world. But, compared to similar substances, it melts about 100 degrees above the expected melting point and it boils about 150 degrees above the expected boiling point. The result is that it is the only material that exists naturally on Earth in all three forms - as ice, liquid, and vapour.

What is even more astonishing is the fact that most of these anomalous properties of water are absolutely crucial for life.

23 WHY DO I HAVE THIS PAIN?

Besides dowsing whether you are taking in the right amount of water, or if your balance of minerals or vitamins is ok, health dowsing can mean a lot more. It can help us find the CAUSE of any health issue and following on from that the CURE. There are both tangible and intangible causes for ill health. Tangible' reasons include:

Not enough exercise;

Not enough water;

Food intolerances;

Toxins;

Incorrect balance of vitamins and minerals;

Wrong food and nutrition.

You can dowse for the cause and what you should

do about it. For instance on the questions of exercise try dowsing these questions:

Taking everything into consideration what would be the best form of exercise to meet my body's current needs...?

Walking...?

Cycling...?

Swimming...?

How often per week...? Once...? Twice...? Every day...?

What would be the optimal length of time for each session...? 20 Minutes...? Half an hour...? An hour...?

And are you drinking enough water?

As we've already seen, Dr Fereydoon Batmanghelidj, world-renowned authority on the health benefits of drinking water, says: 'There is no system or function of the body not pegged to the flow of water.' A reminder: He recommends drinking half your body weight in ounces every day. Dowse:

For optimal health what are my body's current daily needs for pure drinking water...?

More than half a litre...? More than a litre...?

Would my current health condition benefit from an

additional intake of water...?

Bottled water? Tap water?

Are there any significant levels of toxins in this water that would be detrimental to my health...?

More than 10 per cent...? 20 per cent...?

Food intolerances

In today's world more and more people are suffering from allergies and food intolerances, said to be due to stress, work and family pressures, genetically modified crops, pollution etc.

If you want to know what's good for you...Dowse for it. Compile a list of different foods – dairy products, fish, meat, eggs, vegetables etc and check out if your body shrinks in horror when you are about to savour a mouthful of your favourite food. It is said that humans often crave what the body should reject! As a psychic you must learn to listen to your body.

Toxins

Toxins can come from food or water, from chemicals used to grow or prepare food, and even from the air that we breathe.

AIR can sometimes contain methane and carbon monoxide, vehicle and factory emissions, tobacco products, crop sprays;

WATER can contain anything from chlorine, bleach, ammonia and even over-the-counter and prescription medications;

FOOD has additives, or is highly processed or there are genetically modified foods, and not to forget, chemical ingredients in food recipes such as food dyes (RED 40) and chemical flavourings;

CHEMICALS are in every day foodstuffs containing pesticide residue, particularly on non-organic peaches, strawberries, apples, nectarines, bell peppers, celery, cherries, lettuce, grapes and pears. Mercury is especially toxic.

Am I toc-sick? Dowse for the answer:

Is my body currently carrying a toxic load detrimental to my optimal health?

Are there any toxins in my body compromising my immune system?

Are there any toxins in my body which are a causative factor behind my current health condition?

What is the source of these toxins?

(Find a list off the internet and dowse it)

On a scale of 0-10 how toxified is my body currently?

There are 5 major sources of toxins:

Pollution

Mold

Pesticides

Toxins in water

Food additives

Besides the above, ill-health can be caused by vitamin or mineral deficiency. Dowse 'Have I the right balance of minerals and vitamins?'

'Am I deficient in any minerals? If yes, which minerals? (compile a checklist)

How many supplements should I take daily/weekly?

How often should I check my deficiency? Daily? Weekly? Monthly?

Do I need to take any vitamin supplements?

Which ones? (again, compile your own list).

You might be wondering what all this has got to do with honing your psychic abilities. Well, to be a good psychic you need to have a general wellness and feeling of well being. Otherwise, your psychic skills won't work efficiently.

The above dealt with the 'tangible' causes of disease. But there are also 'intangible' reasons for ill-health and these are what the dowsing instrument is especially good at detecting. Intangible causes are:

EMOTIONAL

Anger, fear, grief, anxiety, jealousy, hate;

MENTAL

Harassment, bullying, discrimination, intimidation, pessimism, negativity;

ENVIRONMENTAL

Detrimental energies, geopathic and techno-pathic stress.

The Energy Body and the 'mirror' effect

Some therapists believe that 95% of our physical problems have emotion as their root cause. This emotion can be one suppressed on a daily basis (a bullying boss, for instance) or it can be a forgotten trauma going back to childhood.

The anger, despair, grief or whatever becomes lodged in our energy field and, unless resolved, is then reflected in our physical body in the form of chronic 'disease.'

Trust your body. The human body has an innate

wisdom and a miraculous immune system. As one trainee doctor was told by his professor: 'Your job is to keep the patient happy until he heals himself.'

The dowser/psychic's job is to balance the body's intelligent and self organising energy field. In many cases, nature will do the rest.

Past traumas are buried in our energy fields which will often go on to show in physical effects. Dowse:

Have I a detrimental emotion? And where is it buried?

Is this pain in my back associated with buried Anger? Grief? Abandonment? Betrayal?

Where is this buried emotion located now?

The left side of my body? Upper quarter? My heart? My shoulder?

Our energy bodies comprise three 'invisibles'

The aura

The chakras

The meridians

The Aura or Human Energy Field surrounds our physical body. These energy fields move with our emotions. The bigger and brighter they are, the more healthy we are.

The Chakras are seven vortexes of energy which connect our energy bodies with the energy field 'out there.'

The Meridians are the distribution network in the human body which are fed by the chakras.

Chakra is the Sanskrit word for wheel. They start at the root of our spines and end at the crown of our heads. When the chakras are balanced and energy is flowing freely, a sense of physical well-being is achieved and when the physical body is in a state of wellness, the mind feels good too. Balancing the chakras also achieves a state of mental clarity and spirituality and we'll look later at how to achieve this.

Chakras are the focal points of your life force, or *prana,* and their individual health is vital to your holistic well-being. In ancient tradition they each have their own colour – the same as those in the rainbow, like this:

Crown – violet, represents spiritual connection; wisdom. A weak crown chakra could mean headaches, worry, anxiety, immune disorders, metal and cognitive problems.

Brow – indigo, represents our ability to think and make decisions; represents psychic awareness and harmony. Out of balance it could lead to visual and sinus problems and headaches.

Throat – light blue, represents communication, truth and principles. Unbalanced it could lead to sore throats, communication problems, earaches or infections, chronic colds, thyroid problems, speech difficulties, chronic tiredness and depression.

Heart – green, represents love, joy and compassion; understanding others. If it is functioning poorly it could cause circulatory, lung or heart problems.

Solar plexus – yellow, represents confidence and control; self-worth, self-confidence, self-esteem. Connected with digestive problems or liver and pancreas complaints.

Sacral – orange, represents sexual energy and reproduction; successful projects and relationships. A lack of balance can create bladder infections, impotence or frigidity and problems with the reproductive organs and fertility.

Base – red, represents physical strength and survival issues like money and food. If this chakra is not working properly it negatively influence the legs, bones, adrenal glands, colon, kidneys and spinal column.

Prana is constantly flowing into our bodies via the chakras. Chakras store vital information. When you are tense or worried your corresponding chakra will feel it. Each chakra helps build your personal development. They help you communicate. Each chakra is communicating with all the other chakras. If one is out of balance this can affect the others. They each are connected to different areas of the physical body.

As you can see, a high proportion of illnesses can be caused by unbalanced chakras whose energies are distributed via the meridians which are like invisible energy veins and arteries in a person's body. Chakras can be rebalanced, thus restoring the flow around the energy body.

How is this done? To practise you can try it on a friend. First ask the permission questions, Can I? May I? Should I? If the answer is 'yes' to all three go ahead. If it's 'no' it means it's not the right time for either you or your partner so postpone the session for a few hours or the next day.

Let's assume it's a 'yes'. Get your partner to lie flat and use any of your techniques to get them to relax at least down to the Alpha level. Beginning with the root chakra, hold your pendulum over the area at the base of the spine, and swing it in the usual search position. It will whirl in a clockwise or anti-clockwise circular movement. This is the pendulum adjusting to the frequency of the chakra. Gradually, it will reverse its motion and let it continue to swing until it fades naturally. When this happens the chakra has been re-balanced and you can move on to the sacral chakra. Sometimes this re-balancing can be as quick as a minute; at other times it may seem the pendulum will never stop. Either way, it's best to have the stamina to keep going as this is reassuring to your partner (or client, if you have progressed to being a professional). So, a complete base to crown sequence could take 10 minutes or an hour, or even longer. But, once complete, the recipient will almost certainly feel a sense of euphoria and well being.

Remember, you are only part of the process; another part is the recipient's unconscious attitude – they must be prepared to accept what you are prepared to give. And not every chakra will need to be re-balanced so the movement of the pendulum might be minimal. And remember, closely associated with our chakras are our auras and meridians. All three are what enable energy healing to work. For a bit of personal energy spring cleaning the dowser can help balance his/her energy field by using her dowsing tool, allied to her INTENT. Dowse:

Is my crown chakra out of balance?

My brow chakra?

My throat chakra?

And so on...

For optimum mental health cultivate a positive approach to life. Absence of stress goes well with good health. Love yourself, you are unique. Release your anger and pent up emotions. Regularly clear your auric fields and chakras of 'junk.' Try to bring peace, balance and harmony into your life. Dowsing is a valuable tool for keeping healthy and it allows us to understand the seen and unseen worlds around us. The questions that we ask are only limited by the extent of our imagination. You will find that as you ponder, ideas will come into your head and help you to a solution.

We will be looking again at our energy systems and

their effects on us later.

24 REMOTE HEALING AND THE BLACK BOX

Many psychics have a natural affinity to healing – either humans or animals, or both. They use their intuition to help other sentient life. Some claim that distant healing is more effective than much of the healing done face to face by healing practitioners. This is because time or space doesn't exist when connecting or sending energy via the 'Field.' And as all dis-ease is caused by disruptions in the human energy field the healer's intent goes straight to the heart of the problem and corrects it. Once the energy body is rebalanced, the physical body follows. Our bodies have an inner wisdom and they know best what they need for perfect health and vibrant energy. Given the right stimulus they will reach out to the Universal Matrix and draw on what they need to restore health. And the right stimulus can be you using your dowsing instrument to diagnose the cause of the problem – usually emotional – and, energetically start the process of reconnecting the human energy with the Universal Matrix. Because we are dealing with energies that know no fixed time or place our intent can travel across the globe in an instant. Our healing intent can work effectively across both time and space. To achieve this some healers use a 'black box' to aid the process and this is called Radionics. But whether you use a black box to transmit the healing energies, or whether you just use visualization, the results are the same. It's just that some people work better with a device they can 'programme.' The principles of distant healing have emerged from many years of experimentation, controversy, argument and heartache – these challenges especially accompanied the invention of radionics. A brief history of this amazing art would be a good way to illustrate how distant healing works. And many of its precepts are aligned with those of dowsing.

What exactly is Radionics? According to the Radionics Association it is a method of sending precisely defined healing energy to people, animals or plants, no matter where they are in the world. This is exactly the same principle as 'distant' or 'remote' healing or dowsing. It's worth quoting in full the Radionics Association's official definition:

'The name reflects the view of early practitioners that they were "broadcasting" healing, but we now believe that radionic treatment occurs at a level of reality where there is no distance between us. This is a challenging concept, but it is entirely compatible with modern physics and also with the ancient mystic teaching that at some level we are all one, and that at this level exchanges of healing energy can occur.'

The RA goes on: 'Fundamental to radionics is the view that a living body has a subtle energy field which sustains and vitalises it. If the field is weakened, for example by stress or pollution, then eventually the physical body also becomes weak, leaving it susceptible to illness. The aim of radionics is to identify the weaknesses in this field and to correct them, and thereby alleviate or prevent physical or emotional dis-ease.

'This subtle field cannot be accessed using our conventional senses. Radionic practitioners use a specialised dowsing technique to both identify the sources of weakness in the field and to select specific treatments to overcome them.'

'Tuning-In'

'It is not necessary for a patient to be present for the practitioner to "tune in" to him or her. Something unique to the patient, such as a signature or hair sample, may be used as a proxy, or "witness". This can happen, we believe, because part of the mind of each of us is linked via a universal mind. The universal mind seems to function outside the familiar space-time framework of our day-to-day lives and that is why it does not matter where the patient and practitioner are geographically located. They can be together or many miles apart.'

The RA explains that in order for a practitioner to

carry out an analysis and treatment, the patient completes a case history form and gives his/her consent. (In the case of children or animals the consent of the parent/guardian or owner/trainer is required.) Consent can be withdrawn at any time. All information, say the RA, provided by the patient is held in the strictest confidence.

How radionic healing is carried out

The RA says, 'Practitioners use an instrument to both analyse and treat the physical and emotional weaknesses evident in the patient's subtle energy field. Understanding this field requires extensive study. The instrument serves to focus the thoughts of the practitioner and many types are in use, varying in complexity from computerised machines to quite simple devices. Once the weaknesses in the subtle energy field have been identified, specific healing treatments, usually coded in the form of numbers called "rates," which represent the ideal energy states to be induced, are conveyed to the patient with the aid of the instrument.'

I am quoting at length from the Radionic Association's advice to its members because so many of its principles mirror those of dowsing and, at a different level, the psychic world – time and space are irrelevant, results come through focused intent, we are dealing with vibrations, the healing energies (waves) affect the material world (particles) and so on.

The RA goes on:

What to expect during radionic treatment

'The first sign that treatment is working may be an increased feeling of well being. An improvement in physical symptoms usually follows. If you have been ill for a long time several months of treatment may be needed. It is advisable to keep in regular contact with your practitioner during your treatment in order for it to be as effective as possible. Radionic treatment can also be helpful for those suffering chronic or terminal illness.'

What about children, animals and plants?

'All living things may be treated using radionics. Babies, children and animals respond well to treatment, and using "the box" (shorthand for a radionic instrument) is commonplace in equestrian circles. Note: There is a legal requirement for parents/ guardians to obtain adequate medical care for children, and owners/trainers to obtain veterinary care for animals. Radionics is not a substitute for this. Radionic methods have also been successfully employed in horticulture and agriculture.'

The similarity between the philosophies of the RA and dowsing is striking.

My theory is that it's all to do with Quantum Entanglement - a state of connectedness agreed now pretty universally by scientists. QE demonstrates that all sub-atomic particles (which make up everything in the universe) are somehow connected and that any part of us will remain for ever connected with all other parts. That is why a spot of blood can carry the vibrations of its owner and how 'treating' this sample can affect the whole human being.

25 ENERGY HEALING IS THE PSYCHIC'S WAY

By now you are probably something of a split personality – not quite sure whether you are a dowser or a psychic. The answer is you are both. What applies to dowsers also applies to psychics. In fact dowsing is a form of psychic activity. After learning the basics many dowsers decide which area of dowsing suits them best – water and minerals, archaeology, earth energies or health. For the budding psychic, health is a good specialty so let's look at psychic healing. Those that choose to specialise in health have a whole spectrum of sub-specialities – from dowsing for allergies, food intolerances and supplements all the way to treating life-threatening conditions. If we look at psychic healing in more detail it will give you an idea of the process. But if this field of dowsing appeals to you, I recommend you devise your own, unique healing protocol.

The first thing a psychic healer should do, before

even setting an appointment, is to dowse 'CAN I HELP THIS PERSON?' If the clear answer is 'No' then either refer the person to another therapist, or suggest another day.

But, if the pendulum gives the all clear the next step is to gain the client's confidence with a 'get to know you' chat. Explain that the treatment is aimed at tapping into the body's own wisdom and activating its ability to heal itself. You aim for relief, remission, health, calm and well being.

Now fill in a 'client questionnaire' leading from basic details like name, age, address etc to the main issue the client wants addressed. And beware: the health concern that the client selects is not necessarily the one that is the root cause of the problem. For instance, Jane might believe her depression is due to loneliness but the root cause could be rejection by her mother when she was a child which has led to a feeling of unworthiness, which then went on to become depression. But, use Jane's assessment as a starting point. If in doubt about Jane's sincerity in wanting a cure, muscle-test on the main issue. At this point it might be helpful to apply some Eye Movement Desensitisation and Reprocessing, otherwise known as EMDR. Ask Jane to follow your finger with her eyes as you move it back and forth horizontally in front of her. All the while tell her to keep her issue in mind as strongly as she can. After about 30 seconds, stop and ask Jane to close her eyes and just allow her brain to freewheel. As she does get her to give a running commentary on what pops into her mind. As this comes from the subconscious it will often give valuable clues as to Jane's real problem. Let's say the EMDR has revealed clues of an underlying insecurity. This will be a secondary issue to address. Then get into Alpha meditative mode and let the dowsing tool explore further. We explain to Jane that we will address these issues but first need to check if there are any associated problems buried deep in her subconscious mind. The Universal Consciousness out there knows what's best for Jane so let's dowse to see if there are any other factors which might have a bearing on Jane's condition. They will fall in one or more of five broad categories - physical, emotional, mental, spiritual, or environmental. Or a combination of them. So we start by 'connecting' and dowsing these five headings. Oh dear! We find that Jane is a sorry case – she has problems under all five headings (which is pretty unusual but for the purposes of illustration, we'll use this example). Now we need to dowse through a mental check-list under each category to track down the <u>cause</u> of the issue. To establish priorities, check Jane's energy levels in each category. Remember, the energy body is the CAUSE and the physical body is the EFFECT. Dowsing with the pendulum and percentage chart shows that Jane's levels are: physical 55%, emotional 48%, mental 52%, spiritual 68% and environmental 60%.

The category with the lowest percentage - emotional – chimes in with Jane's own analysis so we use her depression as our starting point. If the original analysis did not match we would still use Jane's own version of her problem. After dealing with it, we would explore the top category disclosed by our dowsing. Once we bring the emotional issue back into balance the other categories could also improve. To track down Jane's self-identified emotional issue we ask Jane to imagine the depression at its worst and than associate it with an emotional event in her life when she felt as bad. This takes some guidance but, eventually, Jane pinpoints a trauma which happened 15 years previously. She had caught a bug while on a cruise and this had led to complications which, in turn, had exposed her life partner as shallow and unsupportive. In discussing this we glean that Jane is also afflicted with self-doubt, despondency, despair, pessimism and indecision. So, as a psychic healer, you have a real challenge on your hands. But you have already dowsed that you can help Jane, so have confidence in what your pendulum told you. It's worth reminding you, here, that this example is an exceptional case and it is much more likely you will have easier challenges to tackle in your early days. If your motives are sincere the universe never challenges you beyond your abilities at the time. So have faith! A good place to start in this exceptional case would be to balance Jane's chakras; this will get her energies working at peak efficiency. Let's go through the process. Jane lies flat and you, her therapist, dowses her seven chakras, which connect her meridians to the cosmic energy flow. In Jane's case we find the following: Root Chakra - weak (a feeling of unworthiness); Sacral Chakra – weak (guilt & pain); Solar Plexus Chakra – weak (low self-esteem); Heart Chakra – closed (sabotages relationships); Throat Chakra – closed (lack of self-confidence); Brow Chakra – weak (indecisive); Crown Chakra – closed (lonely and unworthy).

This mixture has fed into the meridians infiltrating the energy body with negativity. Your job is to now restore Jane's balance and harmony. The process can be likened to replacing a fuse in a blown electrical circuit. Once the flow starts, balance is quickly restored. Using your pendulum, swing it into clockwise mode with a clear intent to restore Jane's inner balance and harmony. As the pendulum swings, your own chakras 'entrain' Jane's and brings them into balance. Now we are ready to complete our energy therapy by using a pendulum or bobber to remove any remaining detrimental energies from the meridians, replacing them with beneficial energies. This is a simple Energy Rebalancing Procedure. I usually swing the bobber anti-clockwise while asking the Universal Life Force to 'Neutralise all detrimental emotions connected with any remaining negative beliefs, thoughts and emotions that Jane might have.' Then reversing the direction of the bobber to clockwise I say: 'Bless Jane with energies beneficial to her complete being - physical, emotional, mental and spiritual and bring Jane's environmental energies to the most appropriate level for Jane's highest good. In love and gratitude, Amen'

You can then check Jane's progress by muscle testing.

Other modalities that might help Jane as a secondary treatment include Energised Water and Signature Essences. All these techniques work because of the dual nature of matter as demonstrated by Quantum Theory. Just as light possesses a dual nature of being both particles (matter) and waves (energy) our bodies are the same. And our healing procedures work on the waves and are transmitted to the particles. In other words, we address the energies of our bodies and their imbalances. All procedures are conducted with Intent and the results are verified by dowsing and muscle-testing. Which of these should we use for Jane?

Energised water

To assist the healing process Jane is prescribed eight glasses of water a day, impregnated with healing resonances unique to her. How? You give her one of two glass nuggets already 'blessed' by you with beneficial energies. You, the therapist, keeps one while Jane takes the other. Yours will be a 'twin' of Jane's and, by virtue of the Quantum Field's Quantum Entanglement, you will be able to 'top up' the energies of Jane's nugget at a distance by topping up your own. Instruct Jane to drop the nugget into a drinking glass filled with water, leaving it five minutes before drinking the contents. This is done four times a day. The positive vibrations contained in the water enters Jane's bloodstream and passes on the beneficial energies to her whole being.

Signature essences

For added effectiveness you can encourage Jane to buy some Bach Flower Remedies appropriate to her emotional needs which she can mix with the energised water before drinking. Probably the most convenient way for Jane would be for her to drop one of her energised nuggets into a bottle of water. Then, after pouring the energised water into a glass she adds four drops of these essences four times a day. To make it easy, she can put the drops into every other glass of energised water she drinks. In this way she will be giving her body doses of water charged with healing energy (via the nugget) as well as the same water boosted by the power of natural flower essences. Note, that none of the treatments is in any way physically invasive and the essences are totally harmless and it is only possible to overdose on them if you have overdosed on water itself!

To enhance the power of this treatment Jane should emphasise the positive intent involved by, herself, carrying out a simple affirmation process, calling on powers beyond the self – it can be God, my Higher Self, the Cosmic Consciousness, the Zero Point Field or however she conceives The Divine. Using a form of words something like...'I call on the Universal Consciousness to bless this (water, healing process, essences etc) with energy to bring balance, harmony, health and healing to my complete being – physical, emotional, mental and spiritual. I ask this in love and gratitude...' Then an Amen or Thank you.

The unique combination of the above procedures have a strong likelihood of helping Jane back to a more healthy and happy existence. To check Jane's progress at each consultation she can be assessed by 'muscle-testing' linked with dowsing for her percentage energy levels.

If jane is not able to be present for personal healing, the

same healing techniques can be used employing a willing surrogate who 'becomes' jane while you carry out the same process as above. as you know this works because of good old quantum entanglement.

26 ...I THINK, THEREFORE IT IS...

As the 20th Century's greatest scientist Albert Einstein said, 'Everything is energy and energy is everything.' Our thoughts and emotions are energy and we send these out to the universe every moment of our lives and what we send out affects what comes back to us. Like attracts like. So, send out negative thoughts ('I don't like him – he's opinionated and anyway he's too fat...') and these negative thoughts will rebound and bring disharmony in to your life. Our internal energy systems are governed by our auras, chakras and meridians. If these become blocked, distorted, clogged up or torn the rest of us physically, mentally and emotionally is damaged. These blockages, distortions, disruptions, tears and other forms of damage can be caused by our own negative thoughts coming back to us or someone else's detrimental thoughts getting through our psychic defences.

As well as toxins and poisons, past life memories lodged in our auras or chakras, can also unbalance our health. And, as we will see later, entities or spirits can create havoc, too. In fact, some contend that our thoughts are actually intelligent entities that 'possess' the human form and use us to carry out their purpose. When we decide to go shopping, or stay at home, or do some deadheading in the garden, is it 'you' having these thoughts or is it a possessing entity that is pulling your strings for its own ends? In fact who ARE you? Are you your body? Your mind? Is there just one version of you? Some believe that most of us are inhabited by several thought entities who are often at war within us, changing our personalities as we react to events.

When Mozart said, 'Tunes just walk into my head' he was right. His mind was a receptacle of music dropping from the spheres. Thoughts are no different. Mozart was a genius because his thoughts were geniuses. Some of us are idiots because that's the way our thoughts are.

Could it be that 'Out There' is a maelstrom of competing thoughts, who take on the guise of spirits, swirling around in their own dimension, bursting through into ours seeking a life within the vehicle of our bodies? When our bodies die do those spirits, who inhabited us, merely re-enter their own dimension and wait for another suitable vehicle within which to continue their existence?

27 WHERE SCIENCE AND

SPIRIT MEET

Dowsing for spirit possession comes under the general heading of Spiritual Dowsing, which is interacting with other dimensions through the medium of our dowsing instruments. It can be seen as a kind of clairvoyance. And yet there is an element of science to it all, too, because at last the world of science and the world of spirit are beginning to say the same thing. For instance 'String theory' claims there are 10 space-time dimensions while the 'Many worlds' interpretation proposes an infinite number of universes. But we say the ancients have always known there are other realities out there. The way I try to keep things simple is to think not so much of dimensions but more as frequencies. All matter vibrates at its own frequency. Even in our bodies, different parts of us vibrate at different rates. Think of musical notes – everything has its own frequency and the whole lot are orchestrated into a unique symphony which makes every human being as individual as their fingerprints. And we as human beings exist in an ocean of vibrations and the ocean of vibrations that exist on this earth is itself whirling through an infinite universe of frequencies. And, as in our daily material lives, those other dimensions (frequencies) contain both the good and the bad guys.

The good guys include: Archangels, Angels, Ascended Masters, Spirit guides, Light beings, Devas.

Among the bad guys are: Demons, Other Dark Forces, Spirit Attachments, Poltergeists, Curses, Black Magic and Astral Parasites. They all exist as energy and this energy has an intelligence - from rudimentary to genius level and beyond. These other entities who co-inhabit our realm interract with us in various ways. And most often they do so when our defences are down through drink or drugs or any addiction, or through illness. Some people deliberately open their inner beings to give spirit entities access - playing with a ouija board for instance. This is equivalent to opening your front door and inviting any passer-by in. In case you are tempted to think this is all fantasy try Googling Ed and Lorraine Warren. This American couple spent 40 years removing and exorcising bad spirits and poltergeists from thousands of families. 'The Demonologist' by Gerald Brittle is their life story (check out reviews on Amazon). So how do we as dowsers interract with the world of spirit?

With dowsing we can:

Detect negative intelligencies;

Identify the type;

ANTHONY TALMAGE

Remove them from people or the location;

Transmute negative energy to positive;

Retrieve lost souls;

Release lost spirits;

What are the symptoms of spirit possession? Here are a few:

- Feeling drained
- Ongoing fatigue
- Acting out of character
- Memory loss
- Icy cold body parts
- sudden illnesses that elude diagnosis
- Insistent voices in the head
- Addictions of all sorts

How do we diagnose a possible case of possession? First, draw up a comprehensive list or chart of potential spiritual infections – demon possession, earthbound discarnate human, curses, soul fragment, astral entity etc. And then ask your pendulum to tell you which on your list is the cause of the problem. Let's say it is an earthbound discarnate human.

What is the cure?

If you believe you have a spirit or spirits inhabiting your

150

being, first get into that Alpha state we talked about earlier and then visualise any dark shadows either attached to your aura or lodged inside your body. Call in your own Spirit Guide or Angelic Helper to assist you and use him/her as an intermediary. Ask your guide to relay everything you are saying and thinking. Let those shadows develop into a stronger shape and then mentally address the entity, through your Light Being. Something along the lines of: 'I am speaking to the dominent spirit among you. I know you are living inside my space possibly along with other, weaker, entities. You should be aware that you do not belong here and are breaking Universal Law by hindering my spiritual development and not allowing my true self to have full expression.' Then, telepathically, continue your dialogue. You will find the entity will reply and, in most cases, answer your questions. If you suspect that the entity is lying to you, ask the same question three times. The third answer will be truthful because spirits cannot lie more than three times. Don't be confrontational. Remember, the spirit's possession of you may have been something beyond their control and they need your help to get past this hurdle in their spiritual journey. Tell them they have a spirit guide who is standing by waiting to take them on the next stage of their soul's journey. Introduce them. Explain the advantages to them of continuing their journey. Suggest there is no logical reason for them choosing to remain stuck in your energy field. Visualise a powerful shaft of brilliant white light nearby reaching from earth as far as the eye can see towards the heavens. Invite the spirit to 'Go to the light' and take all those weaker entities with him. Imagine them all holding hands and walking to the shaft of light and disappearing into it.

Because this book deals with such a wide range of subject matter it is not possible to go into greater detail on this topic.

In the meantime, let's look at a close cousin of spirit release and possession - Past Life Therapy. This and Spirit Possession are such huge subjects that they deserve a book all to themselves – in fact there are already scores of books on both but few that utilise dowsing as an essential tool.

28 YOU HAVE LIVED BEFORE

How to dowse a past life? An account by dowser Juanita Ott, on her website mirrorwaters.com is worth quoting in full as it uses dowsing and is the clearest exposition of this skill I have seen and is a wonderful example if you fancy trying this yourself.

Nita says, 'Several years ago I dowsed a Past Life for my son, Jeremy. This was the very first Past Life Dowsing either of us had done but not the last! We eventually had another dowser confirm the events of this dowse. I decided to offer it here if you care to read it in order to get ideas for questions you might ask when performing your own Past Life Dowsing. Enjoy...

Nita: I figure I will ask when, where, who (male/female), who in family etc. Can you think of anything else?

Jeremy: Not really

Nita: Okay

Nita (preparing to dowse) : Connecting with Jeremy's High Self

Nita (preparing to dowse): Do I have permission to dowse for Jeremy's past life incarnations?

Nita (Dowsed Answer) : Yes

Nita: (Question to Dowse) : Do I have the ability to dowse for Jeremy's past life incarnations?

Nita (Dowsed Answer) : Yes

Nita (Question to Dowse) : Can I connect now to Jeremy's most recent incarnation prior to this life?

Nita (Dowsed Answer) : Yes

Nita (preparing to dowse) : Please research this life now... (The pendulum swings in research mode.)

Nita (Question to Dowse): Was Jeremy a male in this life?

Nita (Dowsed Answer) : Yes

Nita (Question to Dowse): Was Jeremy a female in this life?

Nita (Dowsed Answer): No

Nita (Question to Dowse) : When was Jeremy born in this life?

Nita (Dowsed Answer, using a chart): July 27 1846

Nita (Question to Dowse): When did Jeremy die in this life?

Nita (Dowsed Answer, using a chart): 1923

Nita (Question to Dowse): Where did this incarnation occur?

Nita (Dowsed Answer, using a chart) : Asia

Nita (Statement): Going to get an atlas

Nita (Statement & Question to Dowse): Found historical maps on internet... dowsed each name asking for a location closest to the area of Jeremy's last incarnation.

Nita (Dowsed Answer): Tibet

Nita (Question to Dowse): What was Jeremy's profession in that life?

Nita (Dowsed Answer, using a chart): Soldier

Nita (Question to Dowse) : What was Jeremy's social background?

Nita (Dowsed Answer, using a chart): Rich

Nita (Question to Dowse) : How did Jeremy die in

this incarnation?

Nita (Dowsed Answer, using a chart): Old Age

Jeremy: Married?, Kids?, Important Incidents? Name?

Nita (Question to Dowse): Did Jeremy have a wife in this incarnation?

Nita (Dowsed Answer) : Yes

Nita (Question to Dowse) : How many wives did Jeremy have?

Nita (Dowsed Answer) : 4

Nita (Question to Dowse) : Did Jeremy have any children in this incarnation?

Nita: 22 Children

Nita: 12 Girls

Nita (Question to Jeremy): Important incidences such as?

Nita (Question to Jeremy): Idea's Jeremy?

Jeremy: Name'?

Nita (Question to Dowse): What was Jeremy's name in this life?

Nita (Answer, Dowsed using ABC chart) : Fioug

Nita (statement, musing to Jeremy): This may be hard to get as the characters in the language may not have been our traditional English so I would imagine that we will not get too close?

Jeremy :True

Jeremy: Last name?

Nita (Question to Dowse): Please show me Jeremy's last name in this incarnation.

Nita (Answer, Dowsed using ABC chart): Kaq

Jeremy: Kinda cool

Jeremy: I am quite excited about it actually

Jeremy: Anything else you can think of?

Nita (Question to Dowse): What was Jeremy's basic life energy in this life?

Nita (Dowsed Answer, using a chart) : Gentleness

Nita (Dowsed Answer, using a chart) : Mercy

Nita (Dowsed Answer, using a chart) : Acceptance

Nita (Question to Dowse): What discordant energies did Jeremy experience in this life?

Nita (Dowsed Answer, using a chart) : Cowardice

Nita (Dowsed Answer, using a chart) : Doubt

Nita (Statement) : That is it, I can't think of anything else

Jeremy: What about you were you there with me?

Nita (Statement) : I could check to see if people you know now were members of your family in that life

Jeremy (Statement): Ok

Nita (Dowsed Answer): No I was not there

Nita (Statement, based on a previous dowse): I was a plantation owner in Louisiana

Jeremy (Statement) : Right

Jeremy (Name to Dowse) : What about Tom?

Nita (Dowsed Answer) : No

Jeremy (Name to Dowse) : Adam?

Nita (Dowsed Answer) : No

Jeremy (Name to Dowse) : Tara?

Nita (Dowsed Answer) : Yes

Nita (Dowsed Answer) : One of your wives

Jeremy (Name to Dowse) : Gram?

Nita (Dowsed Answer) : Yes, one of your kids

Nita (Dowsed Question) : Was Dad? No

Jeremy: What the heck, what about Q?

Nita (Dowsed Answer) : Yes

Nita (Question to Dowse) : Was Q one of Jeremy's wives?

Nita (Dowsed Answer) : Yes

Nita (Dowsed Answer) : Tara was your favorite wife

Jeremy (Name to Dowse) : What about Lora?

Nita (Dowsed Answer) : No

Jeremy (Name to Dowse): Joey?

Nita (Dowsed Answer) : No

Jeremy (Name to Dowse): Sheryl's brother, Joey?

Nita (Dowsed Answer) : No

Jeremy (Name to Dowse): Gar?

Nita (Dowsed Answer) : Yes, a friend

Nita (Question to Dowse) : Was Jeremy part of any one significant event in History?

Nita (Dowsed Answer) : No

Nita (Chatting with Jeremy) : So I can't think of

anything else can you?

Nita (Chatting with Jeremy) : I will close this connection if you are done

Nita (Chatting with Jeremy) : I will email you the transcript

Jeremy: Cannot think. I want to do it again though.

Needless to say Jeremy was quite freaked out by the reading…. But immediately wanted to try again. The next time we got a future life! But that's another story.

The dowsed answers were later confirmed to be true by another master dowser who does this kind of thing often.

I hope you enjoyed, I copied the Chat from Messenger and then I changed it so it would be more readable. Added the bracketed comments so you all would understand better what we were doing. Who knows maybe someone will want to try this themselves, and maybe this will help some to get you started. I have started a set of dowsing charts to use to do your own past life reading... I have quite a few made so far as I have been compiling lists for years. It is a work in progress at least.'

So that's how dowser Juanita Ott explains the process on her website 'mirrorwaters.com' – check it out for more valuable info.

If you want to dowse for your own, or someone

else's past lives, you need to prepare your questions carefully depending on what details you want to uncover. What themes are you interested in? Spiritual? Physical? Emotional? Do you want to uncover a past trauma that might be affecting your current life? Are you obsessed about one topic and want to know why? Do you have a recurring dream that might have its roots in a past life? There are obviously some basics that apply to all past life dowsing – the time frame in the past (or even in the future), the geographical location, your environment (town? country? rich/poor home?). Whether you were male or female, what your role was in that life, what strong relationships you had, when/where/how you died, and so on. There are plenty of charts to help you focus on the essentials. Again, check out Mirrorwaters.com for a selection.

Well, that just about brings us to the end of our road to psychic power. By now you will have enough information to decide if you want to be a serious, even professional dowser. Or a serious (or even professional psychic!). Or both.

If you have found this book helpful please consider writing a review on the Amazon site because this will encourage others to enjoy it too.

And when you turn the final page, after the appendices, Kindle will give you the opportunity to rate this book and share your thoughts on Facebook and Twitter. If you believe the book is worth sharing, please would you take a few seconds to let your friends know about it? If it turns out to make a difference in their lives, they'll be forever grateful to you, as will I.

The appendices below adds a bit more detail to some of the themes covered but are not essential to read.

APPENDIX 1 – THE QUANTUM CONNECTION

It's been said before. There seems to be a connection between the principles of dowsing and the world of quantum physics. In fact the more I look into both, the more things in common I find. Early in the 20th Century physicists like Max Planck, Niels Bohr, Werner Heisenberg and Erwin Schrödinger shocked their scientific colleagues with new theories that flew in the face of classical physics. The world they described turned the orthodox, Newtonian model of large things, from suns to billiard balls (behaving machine-like and predictably), on its head. The new field of quantum mechanics, dealing with very small things like sub-atomic particles, was an Alice in Wonderland realm in which the bullet arrives before the trigger is pulled, an object is in two places at the same time and two particles can communicate across millions of miles at a speed 10,000 times faster than the speed of light. No wonder these new kids on the scientific block were seen as heretics. One of the greatest physicists of all time, Nobel Laureate Richard Feynman, said, 'Anyone who thinks they understand the quantum world obviously doesn't.' Fellow physicist Niels Bohr, who pioneered the study of sub-atomic particles, agreed. 'If someone says that he can think about quantum physics without becoming dizzy, that shows only that he has not understood anything whatever about it.' Bohr's contemporary J.B.S. Haldane stated, 'the Universe is not only queerer than we suppose, but queerer than we can suppose.' Reflecting on quantum mechanics some 65 years ago, the British physicist Sir Arthur Eddington complained that the theory made as much sense as Lewis Carroll's poem "Jabberwocky" in which 'slithy toves did gyre and gimble in the wabe.' But the pioneers of the new thinking stuck to their guns and now, over a century later, their discoveries are in common use in laser technology, the transistor, the electron microscope, magnetic resonance imaging, spectroscopy, fibre optics - to name but a few 21st Century applications. But what has all this got to do with the world of Dowsing? There seems to be demonstrable convergencies in both quantum and dowsing phenomena. When we dowsers access information beyond our five senses it could be argued that, in the language of the quantum physicist, we cause a 'collapse of the wave function.' What this means is that the act of observing (dowsing) somehow prompts the energies that are floating about us as 'waves of probability', to become particles, which then assume a shape and become a reality.

And this mystical 'connection' between dowser and target is very like the phenomenon of quantum entanglement. Based on the Quantum Theory concept I contend that the observer (the subtle energy dowser) actually *creates* the reality s/he dowses. Our intent changes the energies around us and conjures form. If true this would mean that Hamish Miller and Paul Broadhurst did not *detect* their legendary Michael and Jane lines at all (see their book The Sun and the Serpent) - by searching with intent they conjured them into being! Perhaps the potential of the lines were there just waiting for Hamish to give them life. And the energies along the lines have been growing stronger as others have followed after. But that can't be true can it? After all don't we 'discover' lines of energy? Or someone's allergy? Through our rods or the pendulum don't we access our intuition, or that 'cosmic library', for the information that lies, waiting to be found, beyond our five senses? Quantum physics tells us...no we don't. Instead, when we say to a client, 'I have found several lines of detrimental energy in your home and some negative energy spirals. I have now removed them and your living space is clean,' we are not being strictly accurate. According to Quantum Theory we dowsers don't 'find' the 'black lines' associated with geopathic stress, we bring them into being. Reality is just behaving in accordance with the expectations of the observer. Whoa! That's nonsense, you say. A client may have had problems in their home, or office, for months or years before calling in a dowser as a last resort. So how could the dowser apparently be creating the black lines they didn't even know existed until they were called in?

Counter-intuitive though this notion is that's what happens, says Quantum Theory. The dowser 'conjures' those negative energies into being with his own consciousness. The fact that they were causing problems before they appeared to even exist is just one aspect of the weird world of quantum physics, where effect can happen before cause. Those pesky black lines have been floating about their location as waves of probability and only collapsed into reality in response to the dowsers' conscious 'observation' of them. This would explain why two dowsers find different lines of detrimental energy in the same location. It's their human consciousness that is giving form to their own expectations. Yet, these lines-that-are-yet-to-be have been the cause of the mood swings, headaches, arthritis etc.

This topsy-turvy phenomenon is simply one element in the zoo of quantum paradoxes at work. This one's known as retrocausality and posits that cause reaches back through time and creates effect.

To even the most easy-going and open-minded of dowsers, this may seem a hypothesis too far. But if, for the sake of the argument, it is possible, it doesn't negate anything dowsing has achieved or will achieve in the future. In fact, some in the science community would contend that dowsers are among the most effective at carrying out humanity's destiny of being co-creators with God, or however you refer to the Divine - Nature, the Cosmic Consciousness, the Universal Mind or the Higher Self etc. We are, so to speak, co-architects of the Universal Master Plan. So what does this mean when we dowse the energies at sacred sites? Is the energy there, waiting for us to discover it? Or is it our own consciousness that transmutes the inert wave into 'something' which we call an energy line? By our intention to find energies are we projecting a part of our inner being on the world around us? Are we working in partnership with the rules of the quantum universe? And what about those wave functions that might have been collapsed by previous dowsers? Does our arrival on the scene just add to the melange of energies floating about the place? Whatever we are doing many leading physicists would contend that we are creating a desired outcome by causing the waves of infinite probability that exist throughout the cosmos to collapse into the shape and form already in our minds. But where did that shape and form in our minds come from in the first place? Did they already exist in the mind of a Creator, who ordained that his plan would only unfold if human consciousness provided the catalyst?

Cheerleader of this hypothesis was the towering figure of American theoretical physicist John Archibald Wheeler, colleague of Albert Einstein and Niels Bohr and mentor to many of today's leading physicists. Famous for coining the terms black hole, quantum foam and wormhole, he believed creation is triggered by our consciousness. As in the quantum world all time is now, past events and present thoughts interact. To illustrate his point he once told a friend, 'The Big Bang happened because I thought of it and I thought of it because the Big Bang happened.' Wheeler, who died in 2008 aged 96, was not a nutty professor; he was greatly respected in the world of science, a large section of which now shares his belief that human consciousness is a key participant in the unfolding reality of the cosmos. In a radio interview on 'The Anthropic Universe' Wheeler said, 'We are participators in bringing into being not only the near and here, but the far away and long ago. We are in this sense, participators in bringing about something of the universe in the distant past and if we have one explanation for what's happening in the distant past why should we need more?' The principle of the 'observer creates reality' is dramatically demonstrated in quantum physics's celebrated 'Double-Slit Experiment.' According to the aforementioned physics colossus, Richard Feynman, it captures the central mystery of Quantum Theory. The Double Slit Experiment was first carried out by Thomas Young back in 1803, but since then variations on the same theme have propelled us further and further into a real life Alice in Wonderland realm. It's almost as if we humans live in two parallel universes with different rules that overlap at the edges. The best brains in the business have sought to explain the seemingly impossible results of this (in)famous experiment, but so far no-one has succeeded. But, its legacy is a mind-altering view of our world. Dowsers would probably find it easier to accept than many physicists, whose only way of coping with its spooky phenomena is to shut it out of their minds. As dowsers we are well used to the concept 'something happens but I don't know why...all I do know is that it happens.' The Double-Slit Experiment is all about energies – the sort we dowsers love. Few scientists these days disagree that everything around us is made of atoms. And atoms are made of energy. This energy comprises electrons, protons and neutrons called particles, which are popping in and out of existence constantly. Scientist don't know why or where they go. They just know they are elusive but are definitely there. If they weren't there we wouldn't be here. A particle is what we perceive as matter of some sort - something with mass – tables and chairs, buildings, mountains, elephants, you and me are made of particles. But a particle is a quantum Jekyl and Hyde and has another self lurking in its being called a wave, which is an undulating disturbance in the world around us. A wave is a vibration of energy. A particle is mass and forms the building blocks of everything we see around us. Note the apparent diametrically opposed properties of each. In Thomas Young's time, quantum theory hadn't been invented. He performed his experiment to prove that Newton was wrong in asserting that light was made up of little particles. Young averred that light travelled through the ether as waves. To prove it he shone a beam through a metal sheet with a slit in it and a vertical band of light appeared on a screen, which had been placed behind the slit. So far so good – just what you would expect. He then shone the light through two parallel slits and, instead of getting two parallel bands he got something looking like an oversized bar-code – bands of light and shade. Young was delighted at this because it proved that the light had passed through the slits as waves because it had formed what is known as an 'interference pattern', and was behaving just like the waves he had created in a tank of water when he conducted an earlier experiment. An 'interference pattern' is always caused when waves spread out after passing through the slits and collide with one another. So far in the experiment, everything had gone to plan and he had proved Newton wrong. Light was definitely made of waves. But over a century later, well after Quantum Theory was invented, scientists decided to see what would happen if they 'fired' particles through the slits, like a gun shooting marbles. For ease of use they employed photons, particles of light. When one slit was fired at things went just as expected – a vertical bar appeared. BUT...when they used both slits, instead of the expected two bars, an interference pattern materialised. How could this be? How could a particle – a little piece of matter - behave like a wave? To try to work it out, baffled physicists decided to fire one photon at a time so it couldn't be suggested that the particles were bouncing off each other and causing the bands. The mystery deepened; an interference pattern manifested itself again. The particle behaved as if it was going through one slit while its ghostly twin was passing through the other and interfering with itself. Now here is where the relevance to dowsing comes in. Determined to get to the bottom of this enigma, the experimenters placed a detector next to the front of one opening to see which slits the 'real' single photon actually went through. The result was beyond their imagination. When observed, the particle reverted to type and behaved just like a little marble going through just one slit and creating a single, vertical band. No interference pattern in sight. It seemed that *the very act of observing it had caused the photon to go though just one slit, not both*. What had happened to its ghostly other self? The photon had apparently decided to act like a particle and not a wave, as though it was aware of being watched. When the scientists stopped watching the interference pattern reappeared! It seems the scientists' minds had determined how reality had unfolded. So, what is matter? Particles or waves? It would seem that both Newton and Young were correct – light can be BOTH particles and waves. Matter exists as waves of probability until the observer (human consciousness) causes, in science jargon, a collapse of the wave function and reality appears. For some unknown reason that haunts scientists, everything we perceive as having mass is just a wave of information (or possibilities) until we observe it in some way. The Double-Slit Experiment shows us that we dowsers create reality just by dowsing for it (observing). So, returning to the original hypothesis of this article. Do we as dowsers of subtle energies actually create what we are looking for? By focusing our minds and bringing our rods/pendulums/Y-rods into play are we causing infinite probabilities to coalesce into one reality? And is that reality a product of our own consciousness or are we acting in partnership with the Cosmic Creator? While it's just possible to believe that in some way we manipulate the unseen energies all around us, what about the creation of physical objects like streams, or archaeological remains, that have probably been there for hundreds of years? Does the same principle – the observer creates reality – apply to solid objects? When we search for water 200 feet under the ground, is the water there or are we creating it? Of course the water is there, you will reply. It's obvious that a stream has been trickling its way across the geological strata for aeons and we, as dowsers, eventually detect it. That is the conventional view. But, looked at through the prism of the Quantum Universe, the stream has only been there for eons because it 'knew' it was to be created by human consciousness out of the waves of a million possibilities. It was there because, one day, you (or some other conscious being) were destined to find it. The Divine Plan is already nascent, worked out in every detail. It waits only for us to bring it to life.

Preposterous? Perhaps, but evidence of this radical viewpoint can be found in a sequel to the dreaded Double-Slit Experiment – the Delayed Double-Slit Experiment. Back to the questing mind of John Archibald Wheeler. He set up detectors *the other side of the slits* to monitor which slit the particle had actually gone through *after it had made its choice*. The results were astounding. Whichever photon or electron detected AFTER it had passed through the slit always behaved as a particle. Not a wave in sight. But those that were not being monitored behaved as waves! The inescapable conclusion was that the particle 'knew' before it even reached the slit that it was going to be observed, so it obediently behaved as a particle. It seemed that somehow it had read the scientists' minds. Or perhaps it was just playing its part in a pre-destined scenario. A variation on this experiment has been done hundreds of times since, using state-of-the-art equipment, including laser beams, beam splitters and a device called the "electron biprism", always with the same results. The 'observation', involving the participation of human consciousness, causes reality to jump into being.

But, is it really possible that dowsers can 'create' such solid matter as archaeological remains, or an underground stream just by detecting it? How could this be? How could the ruins of a Roman palace (and, by implication the glories of the Roman empire itself) only exist courtesy of human consciousness engaging with it some time in the future? Here we come back to the co-creation theory. It works perfectly if you can accept that everything is pre-ordained and that life in this dimension unfolds to a Cosmic Plan, which requires human consciousness as a co-creator. The prescient particle above was not reading any minds. It was merely playing its part in the timeless, cosmic drama. Admittedly, this idea is a tall order for those who believe in the concept of free will. But a universe unfolding to a meticulous plan is a notion supported by science.

Proposing a variation of the above Delayed Choice research Professor Wheeler pointed out that astronomers could perform the same experiment on light from quasars, those extremely bright, mysterious objects found near the edges of the universe. The experiment requires a 'gravitational lens', which is provided by a galaxy or other massive object. This gravitational lens splits the light from the quasar and then refocuses it in the direction of a distant observer, creating two or more beams of light. The astronomers' choice of how to observe the quasar's photons here in the present *determines which path each photon took billions of years ago!* Wheeler's thought experiment has since been demonstrated in a laboratory. In

1984 physicists at the University of Maryland used a light source and an arrangement of mirrors to provide a number of possible photon routes. It was clearly demonstrated that the paths the photons took were not fixed until the experimenters made their measurements, even though those measurements were performed after the photons had already left the light source and had begun their circuit through the trail of mirrors. Wheeler conjectured we are part of a universe that is a work in progress; as it observes itself it is building itself. It is not only the future that is still undetermined but the past as well. When we peer back into time, even all the way back to the Big Bang, our present observations select one out of many possible quantum histories for the universe. So, in the delayed choice experiment either the light 'knew' it was destined to be observed by a human consciousness far into the future, and behaved accordingly, or its behaviour was predestined as part of a Grand Cosmic Plan, in which we are co-creators. Either way, we dowsers are playing our part in the destiny of the planet.

APPENDIX 2 – WATCH OUT THERE ARE SPIRITS ABOUT

There are a lot of low spirits abounding in the dimensions next door awaiting opportunities to partake, second-hand, of the old lusts and thrills of earthly life. Some are activated by malice, others merely mischievous, but they draw their energies from their hosts, or whatever is available in the invisible realm. Low moral ideals (low vibrations) attract these low spirits while high ideals (high vibrations) do the opposite.

This view is strongly supported by a Frenchman who gained a great following in the mid to late 1800s. He rejoiced in the name of Hypolyte Leon Denizard Rivail but became better known, and is still revered by some today, as Allan Kardec. He is considered the father of Spiritism and he had a profound impact on the spiritualist movement.

Rivail was a French educator and philosopher, born in Lyon on 3 October 1804. He spoke several languages, and his impressive intellectual background allowed him to teach courses in comparative physiology, astronomy, chemistry and physics in a prestigious scientific school in Paris. For one of his research papers, he was inducted into the Royal Academy of Arras. He organised and taught free courses for the underprivileged.

In 1854, at the age of 50, Rivail heard of the mysterious paranormal phenomena (table turning) that had taken America and Europe by storm. Despite his skepticism, he was convinced by close friends to attend an experimental meeting where he was able to witness such occurrences first-hand. His intellectual curiosity and scientific instincts told him that there had to be a rational explanation for these phenomena. Consequently, he began soon afterward to conduct investigations of his own.

Using the same logical rigour that he had applied to his work in education and science, Rivail set out to understand the phenomena. He submitted questions to different channels (mediums), in different countries. The answers were compared, analyzed, and organized for inclusion in *The Spirits' Book*, which was first published in 1857.

To keep his new area of research apart from his writings on education, Rivail--on the advice of spirit instructors--adopted the name Allan Kardec, which he was told had been his name in a previous incarnation. In addition to the publication of various books, he founded the Spiritist Society of Paris and *La Revue Spirite*, a journal he edited until his death on 31 March 1869.

In his classic, *Le Livre des Esprits* (The Spirits' Book), he expounded a new theory of human life and destiny. Its content is based on trance communications received through Mlle Celina Bequet, a professional hypnotist.

The book was a blockbusting hit being published in more than 25 editions which are still widely read in South America, Australia and New Zealand. It is, without question or equal, the primary text among Spiritists.

Among the avalanche of information from the Other Side is a dissertation on the influence that discarnate spirits have on living beings. Interestingly, it chimes in with the view that thoughts are put into our heads from which we make our choices.

One actual question and answer session covered this very point:

Q: Do spirits influence our thoughts and our actions?

A: Their influence upon them is greater than you suppose, for it is very often they who direct both.

After hundreds of these sessions Kardec produced a useful summary of spirit communications. He said:

'Spirits exert an incessant action upon the moral world, and even upon the physical world; they act both upon matter and upon thought, and constitute one of the powers of nature, the efficient cause of many classes of phenomena hitherto unexplained or misinterpreted, and of which only the Spiritist theory can give a rational explanation.

'Spirits are incessantly in relation with men. The good spirits try to lead us into the right road, sustain us under the trials of life, and aid us to bear them with courage and resignation; the bad ones tempt us to evil: it is a pleasure for them to see us fall, and to make us like themselves.

'Spirits are attracted by their empathy with the moral quality of the parties by whom they are evoked. Spirits of superior elevation take pleasure in meetings of a serious character, animated by the love of goodness and the sincere desire of instruction and improvement. Their presence repels the spirits of inferior degree who find, on the contrary, free access and freedom of action among persons of frivolous disposition, or brought together by mere curiosity, and wherever evil instincts are to be met with.

'So, far from obtaining from spirits, under such circumstances, either good advice or useful information, nothing is to be expected from them but trifling, lies, ill-natured tricks, or humbugging...

'It is easy to distinguish between good and bad spirits. The language of spirits of superior elevation is constantly dignified, noble, characterized by the highest morality, free from every trace of earthly passion; their counsels breathe the purest wisdom, and always have our improvement and the good of mankind for their aim. The communications of spirits of lower degree, on the contrary, are full of discrepancies, and their language is often commonplace, and even coarse. If they sometimes say things that are good and true, they more often make false and absurd statements, prompted by ignorance or malice. They play upon the credulity of those who interrogate them, amusing themselves by flattering their vanity, and fooling them with false hopes.

'They {the higher spirits/thoughts} teach us that selfishness, pride, sensuality, are passions which bring us back towards the animal nature, by attaching us to matter; that he who, in this lower life, detaches himself from matter through contempt of worldly trifles, and through love of the neighbour, brings himself back towards the spiritual nature; that we should all make ourselves useful, according to the means which God has placed in our hands for our trial; that the strong and the powerful owe aid and protection to the weak; and that he who misuses strength and power to oppress his fellow-creature violates the law of God.

'They teach us that, in the spirit-world, nothing can be hidden, and that the hypocrite will there be unmasked, and all his wickedness unveiled; that the presence, unavoidable and perpetual, of those whom we have wronged in the earthly life is one of the punishments that await us in the spirit-world; and that the lower or higher state of spirits gives rise in that other life to sufferings or to enjoyments unknown to us upon the earth.'

The spirits even had a view remarkably similar to Rupert Sheldrake's morphic resonance:

Q: Whence comes it that the same idea--that of a discovery, for instance--so often suggests itself at the same time to several persons, although they may be at a distance from one another?

A: When you say that an idea is 'in the air' you employ a figure of speech that is much nearer the truth than supposed. Every one helps unconsciously to propagate it.

If Kardec's communicators are right, we human beings can plug into either those powers that are positive and use them to fight off evil influences and control our own destinies. Or, let negative energies have their way with us.

APPENDIX 3 – GETTING IN TUNE WITH THE INFINITE

It is in an altered state of consciousness that we gain access to other planes governed by other vibrations. It is on these levels that psychic phenomena operate. The daily focus of our minds is dominated by the physical barrage of distractions going on around us. But when we shift our focus we become conscious in a different way and open ourselves to resonances in other parts of the frequency spectrum.

Put another way, we have to switch off to sensory information and switch on to the world of the unconscious. Mediums have found that one of the greatest barriers to overcome is the intellect. Successful mediumship depends on subduing the intellect, bypassing the conscious mind. Gaining access to the energy field around us isn't easy. Distractions from our everyday lives build up a shield of resistance which we need to break through.

One method of doing this is to set aside a quiet half hour and invoke a ritual or personal ceremony that lifts you to a higher consciousness and the 'group soul.' In other words create the right atmosphere to enable you to sink into a *deep well of alert receptivity*.

The principal requirements for opening our subconscious minds to those other frequencies are: Total belief, visualisation, emotion, letting go, being receptive and a conducive atmosphere. And it needs to be emphasised that you are more likely to succeed if you <u>believe</u> that you are connecting to a wider cosmic consciousness.

As we saw with the physicists and the Double Slit Experiment the human mind reaches out and influences whatever is its focus of attention. Believe, believe, believe! Picture, picture, picture! What we picture in our minds, if we do it clearly, confidently and persistently will eventually come to pass. Thought is so potent that its projected forms can literally shape that outer reality which we believe has been thrust on us by fate, God or circumstance. But, paradoxically, don't strain too hard to achieve results. Use a gentle wishing, backed by a confidence that 'it will all come right.' Intense willing or striving seems to block the effects.

This notion is supported by Rupert Sheldrake who says '...if something is done with the confidence that it will produce a desired result, and the participant, once he has done this, psychologically puts a distance between himself and the outcome. He is not trying to make things happen, but just trusts that they will.... Such circumstances may provide optimum opportunity for psychokinetic intervention.' A Christian might put it: 'Let go and let God.'

We all have access to the Cosmic Energy Field, but to benefit we must have confidence that we have. Knowing opens the mind to energies right for you. And don't forget, like attracts like so open your mind to good thoughts and good things will happen.

And humour works psychic wonders so laugh at the scoffers. What do they know?

Throw aside fear and worry--instead cultivate determination, persistence, visualisation, faith.

And beware of self-consciousness, which creates a barrier against the Field and prevents it working in your life. It's that left-brain straightjacket wrapping around you again. Shake it off and let the right brain intuit. Don't forget, while the left brain has its part to play, our right brains are our tranceivers with access to the wisdom of the ages and other dimensions. Our lives won't fulfil their potential until these powers are let in.

The very nature of the physical plane conspires to bring us 'back to reality' and away from absorbing the positive energies we're accessing. Submit to the energies and let them purify you. Let them correct the imbalances of mind, body and spirit. Build up the energies that make up you as a human being so that, even after death, they are there intact. Because this earthly plane offers our spirits a unique learning opportunity and what our personalities become here is what becomes our essence as we pass on to the next stage of our lives.

Getting in tune with the Infinite

To say again: accessing the wisdom of the Cosmic Consciousness can only be done by switching off the left brain, with all its preoccupations with the business of everyday life, and switching on the right brain and allowing it to take the stage. All this means is acquiring an altered state of mind. There are a number of ways of achieving this altered state. Below is a selection, any of which might be suitable for you. Each individual has to choose his own way.

Binaural beats

A binaural beat is the brain's response when presented with two slightly different tonal changes in a stereo situation. The binaural beat produced creates an altered state in brainwaves, leading to a hypnotic-type trance or a 'super learning' type environment.

It works like this: If the left ear is presented with a steady tone of 500Hz and the right ear a steady tone of 510Hz, these two tones combine in the brain. The difference, 10Hz, is perceived by the brain, producing the sensation of a third 'beat.'

Research indicates certain changes in consciousness associated with binaural beats. Binaural beats in the delta (1 to 4 Hz) and theta (4 to 7 Hz) ranges have been associated with reports of relaxed, meditative, and creative states and can be used as an aid to falling asleep. Binaural beats in the alpha frequencies (7 to 14 Hz) have produced relaxed but alert brain waves and binaural beats in the beta frequencies (typically 14 to 24 Hz) have been associated with reports of increased concentration, or alertness, and improved memory.

The medical profession is now using what it calls 'brainwave entrainment' in the treatment of depression, low self-esteem, attention deficit disorder, drug and alcohol addiction and autism, to name just a few.

Hypnosis

The father of modern hypnotism is Franz Mesmer, an Austrian physician. Mesmer believed hypnosis to be a mystical force flowing from the hypnotist into the subject (he called it 'animal magnetism'). Although critics quickly dismissed the magical element of his theory, Mesmer's assumption that the power behind hypnosis came from the hypnotist, and was in some way inflicted upon the subject, took hold for some time. Hypnosis was originally known as mesmerism, after Mesmer, and we still talk about someone being 'mesmerised.'

Although people have been pondering and arguing over hypnosis for more than 200 years, science has yet fully to explain how it actually happens. We see what a person does under hypnosis, but it isn't clear why he or she does it. But psychiatrists do understand the general characteristics of hypnosis, and they have some model of how it works.

It is a trance state characterised by extreme suggestibility, relaxation and heightened imagination. It's not really like sleep, because the subject is alert the whole time. It is most often compared to daydreaming, or the feeling of 'losing yourself' in a book or film. You are fully conscious, but you tune out most of the stimuli around you. You focus intently on the subject at hand, to the near exclusion of any other thought. (It seems to me that this is a classic case of switching off the left brain and allowing the right brain to do what it's good at).

In the everyday trance state of a daydream or film, an imaginary world seems almost real, in the sense that it fully engages a person's emotions. Imaginary events can cause real fear, sadness or happiness, and you may even jump if something leaps out of the shadows. Some researchers categorise all such trances as forms of self-hypnosis.

Milton Erickson, the premier hypnotism expert of the 20th Century, contended that people hypnotise themselves on a daily basis. But most psychiatrists focus on the trance state brought on by intentional relaxation and focusing exercises. This deep hypnosis is often compared to the relaxed mental state between wakefulness and sleep (the hypnogogic and hypnopompic stages).

In this special mental state, people feel uninhibited and relaxed. Presumably, this is because they tune out the worries and doubts that normally keep their actions in check.

In this state, you are also highly suggestible. That is, when the hypnotist tells you do something, you'll probably embrace the idea completely. This is why stage hypnotism flourished for a while. Normally reserved, sensible adults are suddenly walking around the stage clucking like chickens or singing at the top of their lungs. Fear of embarrassment seems to fly out the window. But, a hypnotist can't get a subject to do anything he or she doesn't want to do.

Self-hypnosis

This simple technique of self-hypnosis or 'autosuggestion' can be used to improve a person's overall health, boost their confidence or simply as an aid to achieving that 'altered state.'

How to do it

1 Select a location at home where you can sit or lie comfortably in a quiet place and close your eyes

2 Take three deep breaths breathing deeply and slowly

3 Deepen this relaxed state by mentally counting yourself down from 10 to one, imagining at the same time that you are descending in a lift or down a flight of steps, each one deepening your state of relaxation.

4 In this deeply relaxed state, mentally repeat positive statements (orders to your unconscious mind) about what you want to achieve. Be specific--for

instance...'Every time I fancy a cream cake, the desire for cream cakes will lessen...'

5 After a few minutes, tell yourself that even when you are 'awake' your unconscious mind will still be carrying out its 'orders' and then bring yourself back to full consciousness by counting yourself back up: 'Three--I'm beginning to come out of my relaxed state,' 'Two--I'm feeling refreshed and alert,' 'One--I'm fully conscious again.' Then open your eyes.

Repeat this technique once or twice a day for a few weeks. Don't expect an immediate transformation. But, be confident that changes are afoot.

Trance state

Trance states are similar to self-hypnosis. It's where you shut out the clamour that keeps your conscious 'left brain' on its toes, allowing the 'right brain,' intuitive part of your mind to tune into 'out there.'

Using meditative instruments are one of the easiest ways to induce deep trance states. These include relaxing music, the sounds of pan pipes or Tibetan Bells and Bowls and the like.

With your eyes open, focus your attention on any small spot or object in front of you and above your line of sight. Keep focusing on the spot and direct all your attention towards it, clearing your mind of all other thoughts and distractions.

Continue breathing deeply and slowly, and begin suggesting to yourself how relaxed you feel, and how tired your eyes are becoming. And this is where the difference comes between self-hypnosis and the trance state. Whereas in self-hypnosis you use your receptive mind to accept 'orders' to achieve some goal, the trance state is where the receptive mind is allowed to receive whatever is 'out there' floating in the Field.

Sensory deprivation - the Ganzfeld Effect

Anyone who is trying to learn how to meditate, or is interested in experiencing an altered state, should try The Ganzfeld. This is a state of sensory deprivation produced by covering the eyes with half ping pong balls coloured pink, yellow or blue. Meanwhile, the ears are covered by stereo headphones fed with a continuous hiss, or 'white noise.' Without visual or auditory distraction the subject is said to be in the Ganzfeld State.

Historically, Arctic explorers were the first people to describe the Ganzfeld effect. After they had gazed into a frosty field of snowy white for a while they reported experiencing a form of snowblindness.

Further research in the 1930s discovered that when people gazed into a featureless field of vision (a Ganzfeld), they quickly and consistently entered a profoundly altered state.

When Ganzfelds have been tried by experienced meditators, they have described the effect as instant meditation, whereas most forms of meditation require you to focus your attention on a spot, flower, mantra, etc.

While traditional meditation can take many years of practice, a Ganzfeld works for most people in a matter of minutes. (Some researchers have claimed also to have tested the effects of Ganzfelds on psychic abilities, and have found a statistically significant increase in test scores). People have reported using Ganzfelds to achieve the following:

Instant meditation

Self hypnosis

Astral journeys

Past Life regression

Psychic abilities

Guided imagery

Creativity

Relaxation

Self healing & improvement

Ritual

This is one of the methods chosen by the shaman in primitive tribes to gain access to the spirit world and its inhabitants. They would also employ other vision-inducing means including drugs, yoga techniques and sensory deprivation. Rituals, just as effective today, involve creating the right setting to shut out worldly distractions and using dancing, drumming and chanting. The rhythm most effective seems to be two beats a second.

Hypnopompic/hypnogogic sleep

This is the 'twilight' period just before either falling fully asleep or just before waking, when consciousness is in a half-way 'between state' of relaxation. A whole range of anomalous experiences has been reported during the hypnagogic (falling asleep) or hypnopompic (awakening) states, like brief, vivid, and often strange imagery. Some find themselves temporarily unable to move or speak during these periods between wakefulness and sleep.

Hypnagogic/hypnopompic imagery has been associated with reports of extrasensory perception (ESP), apparitions and communication with the dead, out-of-the-body experiences, visions of past lives, and experiences involving extraterrestrials.

Drugs

A variety of drugs, herbs and other substances are regularly employed to induce 'trips' and hallucinations. However, some observers claim that whatever is experienced under these influences can never be the truth and that this is only ever achievable by natural methods which do not distort the chemistry of the brain.

Meditation

This is simply tuning into those 'higher vibrations' by quietening our minds, listening to music or exposing our thoughts to other uplifting stimuli.

Latihan

This is the Indonesian word for exercise, the practice of which, say followers of the eastern spiritual movement Subud, evokes the reappearance of a primordial power hidden within human beings and all creatures. This power manifests itself in spontaneous bodily movements and utterances, a mood of tranquility and joy, clarity of awareness, and love for the Divine.

According to its practitioners it works progressively to cleanse and harmonise the conflicting elements of our being, to heal and to illuminate. Its essential nature is celebration and praise. Adherents say it makes possible an increasingly profound realisation of the Wisdom from which we ultimately spring and in which all things are embraced.

Because this spiritual exercise is entirely spontaneous it follows no pre-existing plan, and so cannot be either studied or taught. It cannot be directed or forced in any way, but is simply received, as a life and movement arising from the very centre of a person's being, in whatever forms are appropriate for the particular nature and condition of the practitioner.

Since the action of the *latihan* is cathartic as well as

illuminating, its manifestations may occasionally be grotesque or unpleasant; more usually they are enjoyable, and at times they are of an extraordinary beauty. But because these manifestations are simply the means by which the believer is gradually transformed, they are all accepted with gratitude and experienced with objectivity and detachment.

Prayer

Perhaps the Christian equivalent of the *latihan* is prayer, when the mind seeks earnestly to connect with its Maker. This can lead to a profound experience known as Baptism of the Holy Spirit, in which the believer is filled with Divine power.

References to being 'baptised in the Spirit' are numerous in the Bible. Jesus emphasized the importance of the experience.

'And being assembled together with them, He commanded them not to depart from Jerusalem, but to wait for the Promise of the Father which, He said, ..."you have heard from Me; for John truly baptized with water, but you shall be baptized with the Holy Spirit not many days from now"' (Acts 1.4,5).

Jesus explained the purpose of baptism in the Holy Spirit thus:

'But you shall receive power when the Holy Spirit has come upon you; and you shall be witnesses to me in

Jerusalem, and all Judea and Samaria, and to the end of the earth' (Acts 1.8).

The Bible makes it clear that baptism of the Holy Spirit is not for the cleansing of sin, but for the purpose of empowerment.

'Then the Day of Pentecost had fully come, they were all with one accord in one place. And suddenly there came a sound from heaven, as of a rushing mighty wind, and it filled the whole house where they were sitting. Then there appeared to them divided tongues, as of fire, and one sat upon each of them. And they were all filled with the Holy Spirit and began to speak with other tongues, as the Spirit gave them utterance"' (Acts 2.1-4).

The experience continues to this day, in particular within the Pentecostal Church. Those baptised speak with tongues and have other paranormal gifts like prophecy and healing. The spirit is invited into a person's life and its appearance is sometimes facilitated with the laying on of hands.

A dramatic manifestation of the baptism experience in 1994 has spread round the world.

Known as the Toronto Blessing it started at the Toronto Airport Vineyard Church on January 20. After a sermon by Randy Clark, a Vineyard pastor from St. Louis, Missouri, people began to laugh hysterically, cry, leap, dance, and even roar as a result of what the church called 'a moving of the Holy Spirit.'

Later, a commentator who studied the phenomenon was more specific about the behaviour of the congregation. He said the event caused 'shaking, jerking, loss of bodily strength, heavy breathing, eyes fluttering, lips trembling, oil on the body, changes in skin colour, weeping, laughing, drunkenness, staggering, travailing, dancing, falling, visions, hearing audibly the spirit realm, inspired utterances--prophecy, tongues, interpretation--angelic visitations and manifestations, jumping, violent rolling, screaming, wind, heat, electricity, coldness, nausea as discernment of evil, smelling or tasting good or evil presences, tingling, pain in the body as discernment of illnesses, feeling heavy weight or lightness, trances, altered physical state while seeing into the spirit world, inability to speak normally, disruption of the natural realm, electrical circuits blown.'

The Christos Experience

Australian journalist G M Glaskin wrote the book *Windows of the Mind* in 1974 in which he described a technique for enabling human consciousness to separate from the physical body and travel to distant locations, both in present time and in the past and the future. His system involves a series of exercises during which the subject becomes progressively relaxed and the sense of body image becomes slightly distorted and disoriented. Next, imagery is employed to enable the subject to perceive locations, distant in time and space.

The technique employs three people, the subject

and two helpers. One helper sits at the subject's head and, with the soft ball of the fist, firmly massages the subject's forehead in a circular fashion. The other helper firmly massages the subject's feet. This continues for about five to fifteen minutes.

Next, one helper instructs the subject in various visualisation exercises during which the subject imagines first the legs extending and getting longer, then returning to normal, then the arms, and head doing the same. This proceeds until the subject feels that he is able to 'grow' at will about two or three feet.

After the stretching and imaging exercises the subject visualises their own front door, taking care to look closely at all its features, and describes what they see. The helper then takes the subject mentally up above their house, in several stages, to visualise the location from different heights. The subject is then instructed to change the time of day from dark to sunny and back again so that they feel that they have complete control of the situation.

The subject is then instructed to fly up above the clouds, to travel and to come down somewhere else. The helper then asks the subject, 'Look at your feet. What do you have on your feet?' Various questions can be asked, such as 'What are you wearing? Touch your hair, what length is it? Look at your hands...' etc.

From then on the helper questions the subject as they proceed through the scene, which may be from their current or past life. Other people in the room can also ask questions. The subject usually terminates the experience themselves and returns to the present and back to normal.

In one experiment involving a class of students some relived parts of their earlier present lives, whilst others seemed to talk about lives which were definitely not their own, either in character or time-period. 'Peter' related part of his childhood in rural Canada, while 'Gwen' remembered part of a life as a South American Indian woman. Each student recounted a different experience.

Enthusiasts say anyone wanting to try the experiment for themselves can do so easily. You simply arrange with several friends to carry out a Christos session, each taking turns to be the experiencer and helper. You are advised to have a comfortable, warm place to work, free from distractions.

When rubbing the ankles and the forehead use light, circular motions. Remember that you can terminate the session at any time. And it's important to remember that if you do not like where you are you do not need to stay there but can easily and quickly return to your body.

The Christos exercise can be carried out with just two people: the experiencer with an interviewer guiding the exercise, or one individual can even carry out the exercise on his own.

Cosmic Communion

The principle at work is similar to that found in Subud, the difference being that there is no need for a 'chain reaction' from one 'opened' person to another. The Cosmic Communion establishes a 'one to one' with a Higher Source.

Its essence, say its followers, is an inner surrender which offers a new means of receiving, from the Cosmic Consciousness, direct and individual guidance for the right conduct of your life. Sincere submission will trigger an inpouring of a gentle power which, if you will let it, will guide you along the path that is right for your life.

The idea is to relax and surrender with patience and sincerity and the process will begin. Your mind must be in 'neutral' to get the most out of the exercise. Contact is made by creating the same kind of quiet appropriate for half an hour or so of meditation. You should begin by standing (not sitting or lying down). Take a few slow, deep breaths and surrender. Surrender your thoughts and desires and invite the Power into your life.

What will follow over the coming hours, days, weeks, months and, often years, will be a gradual but discernible purification--first of your physical being, then your feelings and emotions and, last of all, your understanding.

The process is available to everyone, Christian, Jew, Muslim, Buddhist, or atheist. The only essential is that you must believe there is something 'out there' that is greater than yourself and that in some way believers are able to come into contact with that Power.

The response in your half-hour sessions may be absolutely nothing at first and this will be the test of your determination, patience and sincerity. Some sign will eventually come. However, you may notice your body starting to move spontaneously, following no required pattern as you might find stipulated in yoga, for instance. The movement cannot be directed or forced in any way, but is simply received in whatever form is appropriate for your own unique nature and condition.

The action may be cathartic so its manifestations might occasionally be grotesque or unpleasant. Just go with the flow of the Power. And trust. More usually the movements are enjoyable, and at times of an extraordinary beauty. You should treat the grotesque and the beautiful with the same objectivity and detachment. Trust.

To begin with in your daily life you may find a flare-up of your weaknesses and failings before you will be able to detect a definite improvement.

Preactitioners say what is important in this process is your *submission* to the will, protection and power of the Higher Force, or Cosmic Consciousness, or Supreme Being, or whatever you are comfortable with calling it. The fact is, you are part of an intricate kaleidoscope of energy patterns which have a form and substance and a destiny. Analysing the power which you are submitting to is merely a hindrance as you are trying to bring intellect to bear where reasoning and thinking is incapable of defining the indefinable. 'Be still and know that I am God.'

On offer to you is the same life-changing power as described in the Christian Bible where, in the New Testament, Jesus's disciples were filled with the Holy Spirit. Humble, frightened and confused souls became transformed into confident, purposeful people led by an inner guidance and fortified by an inner strength.

In The Cosmic Communion we receive and experience a working of the Life Force which will change our hearts, our characters and our physical health. Our faults will gradually be erased and what is good and true and real will happen without any help from our intellect, our hearts or our desires.

The essence of The Cosmic Communion is the pure and passive 'receiving' of the Life Force. The Cosmic Consciousness does the work; we do nothing. Only surrender. It is from the effects of our sessions of surrender that all else will flow including, ultimately, a fuller understanding of what is necessary for each one of us.

Adherents say if you can follow this way with sincerity, trust, patience, even in adversity or when life seems stagnating, with a true spirit of submission, you will eventually be transformed as will the lives of those around you.

In this pathway there is no discrimination between

the different religions, because what comes to a person is really what is already there within him. So if a person is a Christian he will meet with the real Christ in him, and if a Buddhist he will meet the real Buddha in him. The same if he is a Muslim; he will meet the Muhammad in himself.

We humans are being corrupted by worldly influences, our desires, emotions and thoughts every second of the day. We are under siege. Under our own power we might struggle to overcome one defect while 10 new ones grow. Followers say two or three half-hour Communion sessions a week is the way to cast out the imperfections and impurities which dwell in our inner beings. And to point us the way to our destinies.

A shock to the system

Sometimes a physical or mental shock, which jolts us out of our normal routines, is enough to overcome the barrier surrounding our unconscious minds and enables us to connect to the universal energy.

Q. If in The Cosmic Communion, or Subud or any other method of contacting a Higher Force we are supposed to submit and open ourselves, how do we know that we are not being possessed by an evil force? How can we be sure that the power to which we submit is good?

A. We cannot be absolutely sure of anything but it is our choice which thoughts to accept or reject as they come into our heads. If we are inviting into our beings only that which is good and wholesome this will protect us from marauding negative entities. And you, and those around you, will also know that what is manifesting in your life is something good and that it reflects what a true approach to God, Brahma, Jehovah, Allah, Tao or the Life Force should be.

From my own experience and observation I am convinced that the power at work is good but such an assertion is only for me. You will have to make up your own mind.

Q: How do I know which method of attaining an altered state is best for me?

A: It's probably a matter of trial and error. Having said that, your instincts will guide you as to which you feel most comfortable with. Choose the top three and experiment.

Q: Even if I do manage to set aside half an hour a day for meditation any calming of my inner being is soon swamped by stress and tension as the reality of life takes over. How do I maintain a state of serenity?

A: The more you access the eternal and the infinite in your quiet moments the more the positive energies of the Cosmic Consciousness will help balance your life.

Q: Quietening down my inner turmoil will obviously benefit me but will it contribute anything worthwhile to the world 'out there'?

A: As your turmoil's replaced by a sense of calm, this tranquility adds to the Cosmic Field and is like pouring oil on troubled waters. The more meditation becomes a routine part of your daily life the more potent this effect will be. Mother Teresa was once asked by an eager young woman, 'Mother, how do I bring peace to the world?' Mother Teresa's reply was profound: 'By bringing peace to yourself.'

Q: Should I direct my thoughts during my meditations to try to achieve specific goals?

A: It depends on your personal philosophy. In Subud or the Cosmic Communion, for instance, the only need is to submit and go with the flow. However, some people firmly believe that 'thinking positive' is more beneficial. For instance In the film *What the Bleep Do We Know!?* Joe Dispenza describes his practice of consciously creating his day:

'I wake up in the morning, and I consciously create my day the way I want it to happen. Sometimes...it takes me a little bit to settle down, and get to...where I am actually intentionally creating my day...(then throughout the day) out of nowhere, little things happen that are so unexplainable, I know they are the process or the result of my creation. We're consciously, from a spiritual standpoint, throwing in the idea that our thoughts affect our reality or affect our life.'

He goes on, 'I have this little pact...I say, "I'm taking

this time to create my day" and I'm infecting the Quantum Field. Now, if it is a fact, that the observer's watching me the whole time that I am doing this, and there is this spiritual aspect to myself, then show me a sign today that you paid attention to any one of these things that I created. Bring them in a way that I won't expect, so I'm surprised at my ability to be able to experience these things and make it so I have no doubt that it's come from you." And so, I live my life all day long thinking about being a genius...and as I do that, during parts of the day, I'll have thoughts that are so amazing, that cause a chill in my physical body, that have come from nowhere.'

BIBLIOGRAPHY

Elizabeth Mayer, *Extraordinary Knowing*, Bantam Dell Publishing Group, 2008

George Applegate *The Complete Guide to Dowsing*, Vega Books, 2002

J S Scott Eliot *Dowsing – One Man's Way*, Spearman (Jersey), 1977

Jean Slatter, *Hiring the Heavens*, New World Library, 2005

Gerald Brittle, *The Demonologist*, iUniverse inc, 2002

Baron Von Pohl, *Pathogens from Earth Radiations* ('Erdstrahlen als Krankheitserreger') 1932

Kathe Bachler, *Earth Radiations*, John Living. 2007

Dale W Olson, *The Pendulum Charts*, Crystalline Pub; 2003

Cleve Backster, *Primary Perception: Biocommunications with Plants*, White Rose Press, illustrated edition 2003

Adrian Incledon-Webber, *Heal Your Home*, Amazon, 2013

Dr David Hawkins, *Power vs Force, The Hidden Determinants of Human Behaviour*, Hay House UK, 2004

Dr Masaru Emoto, *Messages from Water*, Hay House UK, 2010

Dr F Batmanghelidj, *Your Body's Many Cries for Water*, Tagman Press, 2007

Hamish Miller & Paul Broadhurst, *The Sun and the Serpent*, MYTHOS, 4th edition 2003

Allan Kardec, *The Spirits Book*, Spastic Cat Press, 2012 (re-issue)

G M Glaskin, *Windows of the Mind: The Christos Experience*, Prism Press, 1986

ABOUT THE AUTHOR

In his career as a BBC journalist and broadcaster and a national and regional journalist, Anthony Talmage has written his fair share of stories about The Unexplained which piqued his interest in the paranormal. This led him to membership of the widely-respected Society for Psychical Research and the British Society of Dowsers where he learned the art of divining. After establishing the Guernsey Society of Dowsers, he went on to focus his dowsing skills on the areas of Health and Subtle Energies. He now teaches dowsing at the Guernsey College of Further Education and runs regular workshops on both dowsing and energy healing. As a healer Anthony specialises in cases where the medical profession has done all it can but the health issue persists. He aims to bring the sufferer relief, remission, and a sense of well-being. Through all his many years of researching the metaphysical, esoteric, mystical, occult, paranormal, the Mysterious and Things That Go Bump in the Night he has come to the conclusion that The Unconscious Mind is the one factor common to them all. Which means that everyone has access to psychic powers. This is now his mission – to encourage everyone to use their sixth sense to fulfil their potential. Anthony Talmage is the author of In Tune With Infinite Powers and many newspaper and magazine articles.

Printed in Great Britain
by Amazon